Jesus,

I Need Your Help

Marty

Sainthood is Yours

Thrive for holiness

Deacon Dr. Christy

Jesus,
I Need Your Help

Deacon Donald Christy

TATE PUBLISHING
AND ENTERPRISES, LLC

Published by Tate Publishing & Enterprises, LLC
127 E. Trade Center Terrace | Mustang, Oklahoma 73064 USA
1.888.361.9473 | www.tatepublishing.com

Tate Publishing is committed to excellence in the publishing industry. The company reflects the philosophy established by the founders, based on Psalm 68:11,
"The Lord gave the word and great was the company of those who published it."

Book design copyright © 2014 by Tate Publishing, LLC. All rights reserved.
Cover design by Ivan Charlem Igot
Interior design by Jake Muelle

Published in the United States of America

ISBN: 978-1-63418-118-1
Religion / Christian Church / General
14.10.09

Author Endorsement

The author's unique style of writing and his deep love for God, draws you in from the first chapter and creates a craving that won't end until you read it's final chapter. (The final chapter will touch your heart and give you peace}

My husbands love and trust for God is apparent in his daily life and he has been an inspiration to me for forty-nine years. He is a true gift from God and his book will be a true gift to the reader.

Donna Christy(Wife, Mother, Grandmother)

During a spiritual journey of over 70 years, Deacon Don Christy has contemplated many of the difficult questions we all face in our own spiritual life such as "Does God Exist?", "Why did God Create Me?" and "Who is Mary?" as well as contemporary issues facing all people including abortion, helping the poor, financial crisis, and materialism.

During this journey he has been blessed with profound understanding and unique wisdom, which he shares as a kind humble friend and faith filled man of God.

"Jesus, I Need Help!" contains the learning's of a lifetime and will guide you to answers that you seek.

Jody Christy (Son of the author)

"A spiritual perspective on the secular craziness of our modern world and the real answer to our everyday struggles... the simple truth! "Jesus, I Need Help" is about what really matters...God's infinite love and mercy which transcends all crosses we bare.

Deacon Don's deeply moving personal accounts and compilation of powerful short stories hit home and encapsulate the heart. "Jesus, I Need Help" is a divine reminder of those priceless gifts amidst the daily grind...God's love which conquers all, peace, hope and faith in a fearless future."

Dr. Donald G. Kube, Jr. (Chief of Staff)
Dickinson County Memorial Hospital

A lifetime journey starting as a convert to the Catholic faith, culminating in a life of service as a Deacon in the Catholic church, has led the author, my dad, to a practical, realistic, and unwavering understanding of his faith.

Through this book you will find straight forward guidance for the day to day questions Christians often ask themselves. "Jesus, I Need Help," leads the reader to notice the blessings they actually have so as to realize that the help they are seeking has actually been there all along.

Scott Christy, son of the author.

This book is dedicated to my beautiful wife, Donna, and our forty-nine wonderful years of marriage.

It is written for the multitude of people who suffer each day from financial stress and needless anxiety.

The greatest gift that God gives to us is the gift of faith, and the greatest gift we can give back to God is acceptance of that faith. As our president George W. Bush said so well, "Faith is not the absence of suffering, but it is the presence of grace."

That acceptance not only includes a trust with our life and the safety of those whom we love, but it also includes financial well-being and the knowledge that all we have belongs to God.

And so we must face reality, accept the truth, and then act with faith on that truth. By these actions, our lives will be complete, fulfilling, and overflowing with peace and joy.

Donna, you are my special angel sent down from heaven!

Contents

Personal Reflection on the Mystery of the Human Heart

There are some things in life that cannot be explained. God's mysterious ways are but a sampling of the magnificence of creation while the emotions and feelings of the human heart personalizes God's intent.

To ask the question of why the heart is the essence of life is to ask why God even created us to begin with. It is not the heartbeat that allows us to sustain life, but it is the heart that allows life to sustain us.

The heart is to pulsate with blood, pump its mystery of life, sustaining fluid back into our body and then returning back to the heart and repeating its cycle. Is life not the same?

We are created as a mystery. At the moment of conception, our body begins to age. Each day brings us closer to death, and like the precious fluid that eventually returns to the heart only to be pumped through the body again, so does the created human soul eventually return to whence it came.

There is a distinct difference, however, between the heart as life-sustaining and the soul as life-giving. The cycle of life ends when the heart wears out and the blood ceases to flow through the body. The soul does not need to pump fluid through our body to sustain life.

It just needs to exist within the heart and feed our mind with flowing thoughts of love and acceptance of why we were created. That is its sole purpose of existence.

It can never wear out—it is indestructible, pure, simple, and priceless, and yet even the soul someday must surrender itself to the reality of a heart that stops beating. It must then take over the task of the heart, beating for all eternity, never to wear out, and always allowing the love to continue flowing.

What a wonderful gift that God offers to us— the human heart and the human soul—not for us to understand but for us to always search, to trust, and to wonder.

Introduction

This book is about budgeting, but it is also about *God*, life, death, and everything in between. It contains helpful ideas, logical solutions, and easy-to-follow instructions for a happier life by using your wealth wisely, living your life according to Christian principles, and accepting responsibility for your good and bad decisions, both in the past and those which will be made in the future. Hopefully you will also understand more clearly why God created you and the incredible love He has for you.

It is amazing how many people carry a dose of stress and anxiety throughout their daily life, not enjoying life to its fullest because of needless financial difficulties, unpleasant life issues, and struggles to understand the very purpose of your existence.

God's personification is unconditional love, peace, and perpetual joy; and this love should sustain us, bring peace and contentment into our life each day, and allow us to enjoy what is really important. How can we grasp this personification of Christ's love when we are so wrapped up in our own little world of material wants and desires?

Our Lord says it best through the gospel of Matthew 6:19–21

Do not lay up for yourself an earthly treasure where moths and rust would corrode and thieves break-in and steal, but rather lay up for yourself a heavenly treasure where neither moths nor rust can destroy and thieves break-in and steal. Remember that where your heart is, there too is your treasure.

If this book brings back the peace that was lost when you began to have financial problems or if this book and its common-sense approach to Christian values and purpose of living will help you regain the spirituality that you perhaps have lost, then its mission will have been accomplished.

Trusting that God has brought this book to you for a specific reason, I encourage you to read it with an open heart and a mind ready to accept His message.

Till Debt Do We Part

Considering the fact that over 50 percent of all marriages fail within the first two years of married life tells us there must be hidden factors that contribute to a marriage breakup.

There are many people who believe that by cohabitating before getting married, they have a better chance of having a healthy and lasting marriage. Interesting enough is that statistics are alarmingly high for those who cohabitate before marriage. Latest statistics tell us that 83 percent of all people who live together, before taking their marriage vows, become a part of that 50 percent failure rate.

Marriage counselors agree that there are basic ingredients that must be present in a marriage relationship, before that marriage can be successful.

Certainly, good communication skills, relationship agreements, conflict-resolution skills, and a desire for the marriage to work are all necessary for a healthy marriage. There is, however, one factor that most people do not take into consideration that will cause much stress and anxiety in a marital relationship.

A recent survey of 3,250 people showed that 57 percent of those who experienced moderate to severe financial problems also experienced moderate to severe marital stress.

And so knowing this statistics, one can conclude that money plays a very important part of a good marriage relationship.

There are many statistics that support this statement, and though statistics are usually boring, the following stats are quite the opposite.

For example, 90 percent of all large debt created in a family is usually caused by the husband even though most husbands would like to put the blame on their wife. Clearly, there are many wives who are the cause of financial problems in a marriage, but generally speaking, the husband decides large purchases. Quite interesting is that large purchases are often toys, and they are not needed to meet the basic needs of a family.

Examples could be a new boat, new snowmobiles, or ORV vehicles, which can be quite costly to purchase. After the novelty wears off, they are not used very much, but the payments still need to be made.

It is also shown that 90 percent of our waking hours are wasted by worrying about money, making money, or spending money. Considering that most people work eight hours a day, this statistics is very believable. I believe there is a multitude of good ways to use our energy throughout the day, but it does not include worrying, spending, and making money.

The problem with today's society is that a successful person is judged by what they do for a living and not for who they are as a person. If you are a lawyer, banker, doctor, or a person who is considered a professional in specified fields of work, then you are considered a successful person. A person who collects garbage, washes dishes in a restaurant, or cleans offices or homes for a living is not generally considered successful in life. How sad that our society has placed the definition of success only upon the money that we earn and not on who we are as a person.

This year, it is expected that there will be over 1.6 million bankruptcies, not only by large corporations and businesses, but also by the average wage earner. This is an alarming statistic because every bankruptcy has a direct effect on the growth of the economy and an indirect effect on every person's financial well-being.

Some people see bankruptcy as a quick fix and an easy way out of financial difficulties, but in fact, it can cause a lifetime of heartache in credit refusals from lending institutions and personal attacks on one's integrity.

A bankruptcy can reflect on a person's credit record for seven years, but even after the seven years is up, it can still affect your ability to borrow money. There are times when federal bankruptcy protection laws are needed, but unfortunately, the law is abused more often than not. An easy way out is not the best way out of financial difficulties.

Being a certified financial budget counselor and working in the money management field for over thirty-five years, I have learned many creative ways to get out of debt without taking such drastic measures as bankruptcy. Perhaps legally it can become an option, but sometimes, as a moral issue, it can be questionable.

A final statistic that lends great importance to a healthy marriage is in the area of credit card debt. Credit card misuse is the one greatest ingredient in destroying personal finances, and because it plays such an important part in the whole picture of budgeting skills, later I will devote a whole chapter in this book to credit card debt and examine this culprit in detail.

As we begin, let us examine the psychological reasons why a person goes into debt, why they overextend themselves, and why spending habits become compulsive, obsessive, and out of control.

Perhaps the most logical explanation for overspending is called the wants-and-desires syndrome.

In today's society, a person needs a dependable car. This can be called a necessity because it is difficult to travel to and from work, shop for groceries, and pick up the kids from school without good transportation. A necessity, however, does not include a luxury vehicle like a Lincoln, Cadillac, or Corvette. Knowing the difference can mean thousands of dollars in unnecessary spending. Perhaps another good example could be a refrigerator. All homes must have a refrigerator to keep their food from spoiling, but a side-by-side icemaker-and-water-dispenser refrigerator can hardly be called a necessity for a family with financial difficulties.

Another psychological reason for overspending is called keeping up with the Joneses. Watching your neighbor drive a brand-new car when they make less money than you do is hardly a reason for you to go out and buy a more expensive new car. Keeping up with the Joneses can be a very dangerous move to financial collapse.

Clearly, addiction to alcohol, drugs, food, and especially gambling can destroy a budget overnight. In my counseling agency through the years, I have seen clients who have lost their homes, businesses, and entire life savings because of gambling and alcohol addiction. Imagine losing $135,000 at the casino over a two-year period and still expecting to get out of debt in a short period of time.

Though this is an actual scenario, the saddest part is that all of the losses were charged on a credit card with an interest rate of 21.4 percent APR (annual percentage rate).

Another client I counseled years ago had lost eighty thousand dollars at the casino over the same period of time, all charged on a credit card with only a disability income of thirteen hundred dollars a month to provide for basic necessities.

Many addiction counselors agree that gambling addiction is more difficult to treat than alcohol addiction because the psychology of an addicted gambler is far more complex than that of chemical addiction for alcohol. Personally, as a budget counselor and an experienced spiritual advisor, I will not work with an addicted gambler unless they enroll in a GA program and follow the twelve-step guidelines for addiction remission.

Depression is a mental illness that can be overlooked very easily by a trained counselor and accounts for many causes of financial troubles. A temporary relief from depression can be felt by going on a shopping spree, but the results of overspending simply lead to more depression, and the cycle repeats itself over and over again until the depression has increased to suicidal levels. I have counseled several clients who actually considered suicide because of the financial problems caused by their depression.

Though boredom is another consideration for overspending, it is not nearly as prevalent as the other symptoms previously mentioned. When a person is bored, there is a need to get involved in community and church activities. Perhaps visiting someone in a nursing home or in the hospital will resolve the bored feeling and in turn help someone else who is also lonely, depressed, or simply bored.

Compulsive behavior, especially obsessive-compulsive behavior, can cause a multitude of financial problems and lead to unnecessary debt. Some day while you are standing in line at a grocery store checkout counter, you take notice of all the candy bars, magazines, and other cheaper items that cry out to you buy me, buy me, buy me! These items are called impulse teasers, and it is difficult to get through the checkout line without buying at least one of these items—you don't need the calories!

There is another less diagnosed symptom that causes financial problems worth mentioning. Perhaps, more appropriately, this should be called a phenomenon. A failing marriage will cause a spouse to buy items that are not needed and even worse not pay the bills with the money allocated for household expenses. Stashing the money in a secret account while not paying the bills is a maneuver used by many who are just waiting for the opportunity to leave.

The greatest danger in doing this is that often a marriage is reconciled before the partner leaves, and it is difficult to pick up the pieces after the damage is already done. This, in turn, can start the conflict all over again and cause even more problems in the marriage.

A divorce is devastating emotionally, mentally, and physically. A divorce destroys self-esteem, it magnifies an already existing depression, and it distorts financial problems to a degree that seems impossible to overcome.

Sometimes a divorce is described as an emotional separation, compounded by the physical absence of the spouse. A divorce can be as devastating as the death of a loved one. Obviously, this kind of emotional stress can greatly impact your financial situation.

There are several steps that a person can take to minimize financial problems during a marital separation, and first and foremost, I would certainly encourage marriage counseling.

Sometimes there are serious problems in a marriage, but it does not mean it is a problematic marriage. There are many reputable agencies that have qualified marriage counselors to help sort out distortions and misunderstandings that needlessly lead to divorce.

If the differences cannot be reconciled and a divorce is eminent, then very important steps must be taken as soon as possible.

If any credit cards are in both partner's names, it is important for one of you to get your name off the account as soon as possible. Keep in mind that if both names are on the account, it means that both of you are responsible for paying the bill; and if one partner cannot pay, the other will be held accountable according to the law in most states.

I have often seen a situation where the husband or wife have filed for divorce, ran up the credit card debt to the maximum allowed, and then left the marriage unable to make payments. The responsibility then reverted back to the ex-spouse.

When a husband or a wife file for bankruptcy and both of their names are on the account, it will force the partner to also file bankruptcy because she is also legally responsible for the debt.

Clearly, all charging must stop immediately until the results of the divorce are finalized and a complete analysis of income and outstanding debt is completed. (Many individuals who are desperate after a marriage breakup find themselves using credit cards to supplement their income.) This is a very dangerous mistake and can lead to unimaginable problems in the future.

Be careful not to depend on child support, alimony, or matrimony payments when planning future income considerations. Even though the divorce decree says it must be paid, chances are that it will not be paid, at least the full amount.

If you are planning on renting a home or apartment, you will probably have to pay security deposits for heat, water, electric, and rent. This can be the cost of a month's rent in advance and sometimes even more.

All of this can be devastating, both emotionally and financially. It is difficult to do, but sometimes, a single parent must take advantage of the social service opportunities available through your state. Many times this help is temporary, so do not allow your pride to stand in the way of providing for your children and yourself.

Rarely does a divorce occur without push turning to shove, and so I strongly recommend an attorney's help. A divorce can be very bitter, and often a person reacts in a way that is totally against their character or moral upbringing. By having an attorney looking out for your best interest, overreaction is kept at a minimum and anger is controlled on a much better level.

Before signing any financial documents, make sure your attorney explains the consequences of your decisions so you fully understand your rights under the law. Don't depend on your own interpretation of the law or let logic rule your decisions. In a divorce, logic is a rare commodity, and self -interpretation is simply wishful thinking!

Finally, a word of advice for those who suffer spiritual pain and a sense of separation from God during a divorce—God hates divorce, but God loves the divorced!

With God's help and a willingness to trust and hold on to your faith, all personal and financial difficulties can be remedied.

We are not human beings having a human experience— we are spiritual beings having a human experience.

Toxic Credit Card Problems

If we were to assign a dollar value, the sum total of financial degradation would be small compared to the dollar value of credit card debt.

Today in the United States, there are more than seventy major credit card companies who write off more than one million dollars a month in bad debt. These companies still make profits of hundreds of millions of dollars each year.

The credit card industry today is the number one cause for the 1.6 percent million bankruptcies each year. You are important as a consumer only when you keep your payments current each month. Watch how fast your importance as a VIP customer will diminish after you become delinquent a few times!

Let us examine this world of credit card debt and see if we can put into perspective the dangers of owning a credit card when moderation and responsibility is lacking in your life choices.

It is very difficult in today's world to get along without a credit card. Even when a person wants to make reservations at a motel, they must give a credit card number in order to have the room reserved. In an emergency situation, such as a car breakdown, a credit card can be a lifesaver and prevent a great deal of unnecessary stress and anxiety. A credit card can even provide a safer way to travel because a person does not have to carry a large sum of cash on their person to still be protected in case of extraordinary circumstances.

All of these reasons for owning a credit card are legitimate and make a good case for credit card use. The abuse of a credit card, however, can be a very serious matter and cause far more anxiety than not having one. Case in point.

I have decided that I want to buy a widescreen TV for two thousand dollars. It is easy to convince my spouse that we can afford this TV because we are going to put it on our credit card and pay the minimum monthly payment, which is usually two percent of the unpaid balance.

Simple math shows us that 2 percent of two thousand dollars requires a payment of forty dollars. Perhaps a forty-dollar payment doesn't sound like a large amount to pay each month, but we need to consider all of the hidden factors involved. For example, an average interest rate on many credit cards is 19.9 APR (annual percentage rate). If we break that percent down to a monthly rate, it becomes 1.65 percent of interest on the unpaid balance.

A fast calculation shows interest being paid each month on a two-thousand-dollar charge of thirty-three dollars. Considering our payment of 2 percent on the unpaid balance, we would be making a payment of forty dollars. If we subtract the thirty-three dollars in interest, we are only paying seven dollars on the principal in a given month.

This does not take into consideration that if a person's payment is late, they will be charged an average late fee of thirty-nine dollars. If the late fee causes a person to exceed their credit limit, the credit card holder will pay an additional thirty-nine dollars in overlimit fees. My calculations tell me it is possible to make a forty-dollar payment and increase your debt load that month by seventy-one dollars! One does not have to be a rocket scientist to see the danger here!

For many individuals who do not use their credit card responsibly, it would be literally impossible to get out of debt at this rate. It is important to keep in mind that I have given you an example using only one credit card. Statistics tell us the average consumer today has eight credit cards with an average debt of $8,574.00. Because of budgeting irresponsibility, late fees, and overlimit fees, along with high interest rates, financial devastation is evident.

There is another danger that exists with credit card use, and it is low introductory rates offered by credit card companies.

The more often a person opens an account with a credit card company, the more often it is reflected in a person's credit rating; and by taking advantage of introductory rates and combining total debt from several credit cards into one monthly payment with a new credit card company, a person's credit rating can actually be damaged.

There are also many hidden factors that aren't entered into the equation. For example, if one payment is late, the interest rate will rise considerably and could very well turn out to be higher than your old credit card. A person must also check the interest rate being paid from cash withdrawal because more often than not, the interest rate for cash withdrawal can be over 26 percent.

As a budget counselor, I have seen many clients who have several credit cards, some for department-store use, others for gas purchasing, and some for general-purpose use. It is not necessary to have various credit cards for different uses. For example, a Visa or MasterCard can be used at any department store or gas station. Why would a person have four or five credit cards and make four or five payments per month when one credit card does what five will do? A person only increases his chances for late fees, overlimit fees, or mistakes that could cost a lot of money in fees (headache time!).

And so we can conclude from the above common examples that credit cards can be good, but if used incorrectly, they can be a dangerous tool in leading us to financial disaster.

Don't build God around your day—build your day around God.

I Am Worth It

It takes a lifetime to build a good reputation, but it only takes a moment to destroy it. That is why it is so important to protect your credit in your younger years. As you grow older, your credit history follows you; and though it doesn't seem to be as important at a young age, it can become very important as you mature and your needs become greater.

Let's examine the ways that your credit history can affect you and what you can do to establish good credit, repair bad credit, and still succeed with no credit.

Credit worthiness affects a person's ability to borrow money or make purchases without having cash available. Many employers require a credit check, and if your credit is tarnished, it could mean the difference between getting a job you want or having to settle for a mediocre job that does not require a security clearance or the ability to be bonded or the security that we look for in full-time employment.

Some employers will feel that a person who has credit problems, coupled with heavy debt, is more likely to compromise his honesty and integrity, especially if he has responsibilities of handling large amounts of money.

There is no doubt that a person will have to pay higher interest rates if their credit history is bad. A person with bad credit carries a higher risk of trust while a person with a good credit rating automatically amplifies his integrity and honesty. Credit card interest rates for those with bad credit can be double the normal rate and extend the payoff time by months or even years.

It is also more difficult to rent a home from a landlord who pulls up a credit bureau report. Experienced landlords will often turn down a person with bad credit and rent to someone with good credit. (It is no different than a person's reputation!) Integrity and honesty breeds trust while lack of these qualities will breed skepticism and doubt.

Though I personally use my credit card for emergency purposes, I find I must sometimes use it for convenience. It is rare for a hotel to accept reservations without the security of a credit card. The same is true for renting a car. I do not know of any car rental companies who will rent a car to a person who does not have a credit card, even if he wants to pay cash up front. The credit card gives a sense of security to those who sell a product and want to be assured of getting paid should an accident occur while leasing the car.

A credit record has more information in it than most people realize, and when a credit report is requested, it will provide personal information about the person who is seeking credit. This information could be a person's name, date of birth, spouse's name, current address, social security number, and other identifying information that is usually asked for on standard forms.

It is also common to supply employment background information such as number of years on the job, title, current employer, experience, public record information such as nonpayment of child support, bankruptcies, lawsuits, past felony convictions, etc.

A credit report should never contain personal information about religious beliefs, a list of family relatives or friends, nor should it contain personal medical records or political preferences.

Frequently, a mistake will be found in a person's credit report. That can be very serious, especially if not found and corrected immediately and will clearly affect a person's borrowing ability. Sometimes, there are legitimate reasons why a person's credit has been damaged. An example could be divorce or severe medical problems. When that happens, a person has the legal right to write a hundred-word-or-less explanation of the extenuating circumstances that have caused the poor credit history.

Whenever a credit report is requested by a lending institution, that explanation must be included in the information provided by the credit bureau. Sometimes, this explanation will allow a person to obtain credit even though their credit history is tarnished.

The following is a sample letter of an effective way to help creditors understand why you might be having credit problems. It is not printed in this book to be used as is, but it can be a guide to helping you write your own explanation. Remember, you should stick to the facts only. Do not include emotional ideas about stress, anxiety, etc. because creditors are only interested in facts. *It is to be a hundred words or less, plus or minus.*

Example of a Letter

Credit Reporting Agency
135 No Where Street
PO Box IOU
Anywhere, USA
Date

To whom it may concern,

I have had excellent credit in the past and have never been late with payments to any lending institution. My damaged credit is a result of a bitter divorce where my ex-husband insisted on filing bankruptcy even though I was strongly apposed. (After he filed bankruptcy, creditors came after me.)

After my divorce, my income was $240 per month, and I had to support four children. My ex-husband is an alcoholic and has not worked for three years, so I have not been able to collect child support.

I am now working full-time. I have established a good credit rating with several creditors and can provide creditable references.

Sincerely yours,
Mrs. Good Credit Risk

One would be very surprised how this short letter will help you obtain credit with a lending institution and begin your journey to fiscal trust and financial integrity.

Lust can't wait to receive, love can't wait to give.

Paralyzed with Fear

One of the greatest deterrence for a person having financial trouble and not seeking help is the reality of what they might hear by talking to a professional counselor. Fear seems to paralyze a human being when he or she is faced with the truth. This fear requires a change in lifestyle or acceptance of responsibility. I have personally experienced this kind of fear myself, and it wasn't until I allowed God to be in control that I finally found peace regarding my stress with finances.

This following is a true and personal story, which seems to illustrate a new perspective for those who are struggling with meaning and purpose in their life (taken from my first book called *Jesus and Mary: A Journey to Peace*).

One morning, several years ago, I drove my wife to work and then headed back toward my office to begin a new day. It was a beautiful morning, and the sun was shining. Music from the '60s was playing on the radio, and I joined in the singing of an old Elvis favorite.

As I pulled onto a four-lane highway, I noticed a truck swerving a little into the right lane. As the driver applied the brakes, something jumped into the air and then settled down in the same spot it first appeared. As I approached the same area, I noticed a bird standing in the middle of the yellow dividing line, and my car caused it to be sucked into the air in the same manner as the truck ahead of me. As I drove past, I saw it was a beautiful blue jay, and I knew it would be killed if it stayed where it was much longer.

Surprisingly, I felt a great need to turn my car around and see if I could save this bird though I knew it was dangerous to stop in the middle of a highway, especially just to save a bird that was probably severely hurt and would die anyway. I turned around at the next block and headed back toward the blue jay, saying to the Lord, "If this is what you want me to do, please take care of it for a while longer." I could visualize the smile on our Lord's face as I told him what to do so this bird could be saved. (I wonder how many times in my life I have told Jesus how to handle a situation.)

As I entered the highway, I noticed another truck headed in the same direction. I was sure the bird would not survive another truck passing by it so closely, but to my amazement, the blue jay did not move. I stopped my car, reached out, and picked the bird up, noticing that all cars behind me had mysteriously disappeared for that moment.

As I wrapped my hands around the bird's body, it started to squeal and cry in a high-pitched voice. Perhaps the bird would have rather remained on the road than be captured by a scary-looking man like myself. Its little heart was beating so fast I expected it to explode at any moment, but it quieted down as I stroked its head and talked softly, telling the bird I would not hurt it.

I decided to drive to my home and release it in a large oak tree in my backyard rather than just on the side of the road, thinking it would be safer there.

After I drove up my driveway, got out of the car, and walked to a large tree, I expected the bird to fall as I placed it on a limb. Instead, it stood on both legs as if nothing was wrong. I watched and listened in amazement as this little ball of color started to sing at the top of its lungs. Tears filled my eyes as I watched it jump into the air and fly higher into the trees. As it looked down from the safety of the large oak tree, it seemed to say, "Thank you for the gift of life."

As I drove out of my driveway and headed back to my office, I realized this gentle animal would have died had I not driven by at that moment and decided to pick it up. It became obvious that God wanted this bird alive so it could bring more joy into the lives of those who would take the time to listen to its song and gaze upon its beauty.

As I continued driving to work, I thought about the experience I just had, not realizing that Christ had taught me a lesson I would share with others many times in the future. That night I shared this experience with my wife, and her tears told me how deeply she was touched. A little creature like a bird had given my wife and me a chance to share and discuss how precious life is to God and every human being blessed enough to be born into this beautiful world.

The next day presented a multitude of problems in my office and personal life, and in comparison to the day before, it was quite stressful. It all began when I drove out of my driveway and realized I had a flat tire. While attempting to change the tire, I found the spare was also flat and that meant I had no way of getting to work on time. I probably would have handled it fairly well if that was all that happened that day, but I am sorry to say this was not the case. It seems my tire was not only flat, but the tie rod end was also dangerously worn and needed to be replaced. By the time I got my truck back from the repair shop, it cost me $350.00, and all was not done. The repair man informed me that the universal joint needed replacing soon and that would cost an additional $300.00. All of this before noon, and I had only been out of bed for four hours.

Later that day, I received a call from my boss telling me I had to travel to Detroit for a special management meeting, which happened to fall on my thirtieth wedding anniversary. This would be the first time in thirty years that my wife and I wouldn't be together for our anniversary, and I was devastated to think that I had to cancel our plans for the celebration. (An anniversary with your soul mate and your greatest love is not to be taken lightly.)

Finally, after the day ended, I headed for home feeling tired, angry, and extremely frustrated. I couldn't wait to take my shoes off, relax, and read the newspaper. It was only when I walked into my home that I realized the day's frustrations had not ended.

I heard a rushing noise in my basement, and as I walked down the steps, I could see water about two inches deep on my new carpeting and a continual stream coming out of the pipe above the bathroom.

A broken water pipe, wet carpeting, a tired and angry man, and all the work to repair the leak proved to be too much for me. I lashed out at God, asking him what he was trying to do to me this day and that I had just about enough of his tactics.

Can one imagine how I acted when my wife came home from work a little later? I was not worth knowing as a human being, and the one person who loves me the most got the aftereffects of my frustrations. Anger and fear seemed to have taken over my life, and all my energy was being wasted on this fear and anxiety. I thought of what had happened the day before and how the bird I had saved was very much like I was at that moment.

I am convinced the bird had stayed in the middle of the road even though it placed itself in terrible danger because it was paralyzed with fear, and its natural instinct would not allow it to react accordingly. Even though it was not hurt and could have flown away at any time, it remained on the road because it was afraid to move!

In many ways, at that moment, I was very much like the bird I had saved. I had become ineffective as a counselor, nonproductive as a worker, and diminished as a human being. I chose to spend all my energy on the fear of losing money from the car repair and what still needed to be done in repairs rather than concentrate on the trust that I had previously had with Christ. How easy it is to lose sight of what is really important in life and to wallow in our own lack of trust and self-pity as soon as something goes wrong.

I now understand why God allowed me to have this experience. I was to learn what fear could do to an otherwise average trusting Christian. Our lives are so wrapped up in ourselves, our minds filled with worry about the future and what it might bring, and we get so inundated with self-pity and greed that we become paralyzed with life.

In Matthew 6:22–34, our Lord tells us,

> The eye is the lamp of the body, so then; if your eye is clear, your whole body will be full of light. But if your eye is bad, your whole body will be full of darkness. If then, the light that is in you is darkness, how great is the darkness! No one can serve two masters; for either he will hate the one and love the other, or he will be devoted to one and despise the other. You cannot serve God and wealth.
>
> For this reason I say to you, do not be worried about your life, as to what you will eat or what you will drink; nor for your body, as to what you will put on. Is not life more than food, and the body more than clothing? Look at the birds of the air, that they do not sow, nor reap nor gather into barns, and yet your heavenly Father feeds them. Are you not worth much more than they? And who of you by being worried can add a single hour to his life?
>
> And why are you worried about clothing? Observe how the lilies of the field grow; they do not toil nor do they spin; yet I say to you that not even Solomon in all his glory clothed himself like one of these. But if God so clothes

the grass of the field, which is alive today and tomorrow is thrown into the furnace, will He not much more clothe you?

You of little faith! Do not worry then, saying, "what will we eat?" or "what will we drink?" or "what will we wear for clothing?" For the Gentiles eagerly seek all these things, for your heavenly Father knows that you need all these things. But seek first His kingdom and His righteousness, and all these things will be added to you. So do not worry about tomorrow, for tomorrow will care for itself. Each day has enough trouble of its own.

I have shared this experience because I believe it was a gift from God, a lesson to be learned and an opportunity to understand that our Lord is always in control and uses unique ways of showing his love to us.

Some children walk at an early age while others seem to take a longer time for that first step. The child is afraid to take the first step, and yet he knows that if he puts one foot ahead of the other, he will move from one location to another. Finally, the fear becomes less than the desire to walk, and a child takes his first step. The fear that prevents this child from walking at an earlier age has suddenly disappeared, and the bumps and bruises become secondary to his own created motion.

So too we humans sometimes become paralyzed with the fear of losing a job or what would happen if everything we owned were destroyed by fire or a violent storm. Tragedy can suddenly change our life forever and cause us to step out of our own little comfort zone and make changes that we do not feel comfortable with. That is the definition of fear, and it can paralyze us!

Fear can be experienced in and from many ways and not just from the loss of material possessions. It can have a profound and lasting effect as we mature into adults.

Another experience with fear that I remember well as a young child deals with a homeless man whose presence in my home one evening changed my life forever. Despair, hopelessness, a stranger, and unconditional love—a strange story to be printed in a book about finances for sure, but it clearly explains God's words: "Whatever you do for the least of My brothers, you do unto Me."

Ignorance of the Bible is ignorance of God.

Christ in the Eyes of the Poor

Jesus tells us that we are his sheep, and he is our shepherd. Sometimes we scatter and wander from the flock as we sometimes wander and scatter from the church or even from Jesus himself.

The Good Shepherd still continues to search for us until we are found, and then with outstretched hands, he wraps his arms around us, rejoicing that we are found.

As a little boy, I can remember homeless people (we called them hobos) stopping at our home many times and asking for a quarter or a sandwich to eat. Sometimes my parents would give them a meal, sometimes a dollar, but never a refusal!

Those who stopped by were always ragged-looking and dirty, with ripped clothes and worn-out shoes. Even as a child, I can remember my heart breaking as I looked at these poor and helpless lost souls, never really understanding what being homeless meant.

This one particular evening, I remember a man stopping at our home and asking for a sandwich. Instead of making this man a sandwich, my parents invited him into our home and asked him to sit down with the whole family to eat a hot freshly cooked beef roast dinner.

The hobo couldn't imagine the generosity shown to him on that day, but his tears told me that he had not experienced this much love for a long time, if ever! Before he left our home, my parents gave him a used but still serviceable wool coat from our never-would-I wear-that! wardrobe.

It was also common for any hobo who was treated with respect at a particular home to mark that house in some secret manner that always told others it was a good place to stop. It was never a surprise to see the same hobo at least two or three times during the winter months as they knew a good thing when they found it. What is so unusual about this homeless stranger is that we never did see this man again!

I am certain, now that I am a little older and wiser, that Jesus visited my home that day in the disguise of a stranger. Through the love in a stranger's eyes and the humility of a homeless man, I learned the gift of agape and the meaning of "What ever you do for the least of My brothers, you do unto Me"—thank you, Lord!

In the eyes of many, Jesus was a strange man! He helped others in ways that most of us would find distasteful and gross. "I was hungry and you gave me to eat, thirsty and you gave me to drink, a stranger and you allowed me to visit you, naked and you clothed me." Jesus was a friend of the con artist, the pushovers, the meek, and the lowly. He was a lover of the lost and lowly, of the decaying lepers, of the skeletal bodies of the sick and dying. He was even friends with the tax collectors and prostitutes! I often ask myself how anyone could love that much!

This kind of love is what Jesus expects from us each and every day of our lives. When we treat the poor with dignity and respect, we continue to prove the existence of God and that he lives in the hearts of the poor. (It is not a sin to be poor, but it is a sin to ignore the poor!)

Like the hobo who visited my home that cold winter day and never returned again, we also need to realize the blessings that come to us through the presence of the poor. Only then will we be able to understand that our constant fear of losing our material possessions is a needless and gross expenditure of wasted energy. Mother Theresa of Calcutta, India, said it best when she described the poor as "the nobility of heaven."

As a child, I often feared that someday I would be homeless like the stranger. As an adult, I came to understand the meaning of life and the gift of faith that allows me to live without fear. It took a long time for me to get there, but finally I understood that money cannot buy what is most important in life.

As I sit in the background and watch my grandchildren giggling while they play on the floor in front of the fireplace, or observe my wife's smile as she teaches my granddaughters how to make cookies (never upset about the kitchen looking like a disaster area with flour on the floor and chocolate smeared on the refrigerator), I know what is priceless! Money cannot buy these moments!

The road to holiness is when you love the person whom you dislike as much as God.

Holocaust in the Twenty-First Century

I would like to shift gears for a moment and address a few issues that clearly affect our progress in finding and living a peaceful and fulfilling life.

It would be wrong to think that budgeting and financial matters are a separate issue from all of the other life-changing events we experience in our struggle to adult maturity. (This is distorted thinking.)

In fact, by not understanding how morality and Christian attitudes affect the decisions we make in life, one cannot face and/or resolve the major trials and crosses we must carry during our brief existence here on earth.

One of the most controversial topics in our society today is the issue of abortion. It is an issue that explodes with emotion, with anger, with uncertainty, and with genuine ignorance of morality by lawmakers, our constitution, and the intrinsically evil parenthood agenda that disguises human creation and promotes evil actions.

It is easier to call the fruit of a pregnancy a fetus than it is to call it a baby. (Doesn't sound so human, does it!) It is easier to claim a mother's "right to choose" than it is to say she has a right to murder her baby. And, finally, it is easier and more convenient to abort the unwanted baby than face the inconvenience of raising a child. (Hypocrisy and selfishness at its best.)

I want to make it very clear that I do not pretend for a moment that this is not a very difficult issue and that the ideas and thoughts about abortion are as varied and different as the people who express them, but I feel compelled as a Christian and as an ordained deacon to address the issue in this book. After all, this is a book about life issues and how to find peace in a dangerous and difficult world.

One day, I was reading an article written by Father Pavone, a much respected and learned man of God. I was deeply touched by his words about abortion, and though many of his ideas are presented in the following sentences, there are some ideas interjected with my own thoughts about this evil act.

Father says the sacredness of every human creation that comes from God is a miracle in itself, touched by holiness, protected by the "law," and concealed through the unspoken but priceless gift of faith in a Creator.

Father Pavone goes on to ask how many readers of this article have a son named Michael or a daughter named Mary. What if you heard that a new law was just passed that said anyone named Michael or Mary must be put to death? Certainly you would protest the law and say it was wrong! What about those who were not named Michael or Mary? Wouldn't we all come together in protest to restore legal protection to all Michaels and Marys?

Clearly, we would say this new law was against the constitution, which claims to protect the rights of all people, and we would never allow it to become a law. Suppose, however, that even the constitution were changed to say that it was okay to kill all Michaels and Marys. Would we then say it was okay, or would we still be outraged and say it was wrong!

In other words, there is a right and a wrong, no matter what the laws or constitution says! Every law must obey a higher law, and that higher law comes from God who says that every human person, no matter what his/her background or condition is, has the right to life.

This is the basis of a civilized world, and it rests on this truth. It is not a question of *our* morality or *their* morality, old morality or \new morality, but rather of *morality* itself! Killing the innocent is wrong, and no law or constitution can ever make it right!

Maybe this sounds far-fetched, but let us remember what happened in Nazi Germany. The power of the state, under Hitler, declared that these human beings were not persons and therefore could be exterminated, which resulted in millions of ethnic groups, mainly Jews, being slaughtered.

A few years ago in Bosnia, the former Yugoslavia, the government decided that Croatian people needed to be cleansed from their country, and over one million were slaughtered. We all said this kind of atrocity could never happen again, but it did, and all of us were a part of it! Did you protest this slaughter, or did you watch it happen, oblivious to the suffering and death? Did you even care?

Now let us change the name Michael or Mary to *Preborn Baby* and look at what the Supreme Court said on January 22, 1973: Boys and girls in their mother's wombs are not considered persons under the law and therefore can be destroyed by abortion.

Since this date, 11/2 million babies a year have been aborted. That totals over 53 million babies who have died as a result of this law, and that number is far greater than those destroyed under Hitler.

When a child is a victim of abortion, we are all victims!

Life is a gift from God and should only be taken by God.

If we tolerate the killing of innocent babies, why shouldn't we kill an unwanted grandparent or an innocent unwanted neighbor who is old and costly to support with our tax dollars? Do you realize that we now have some states that have already legalized euthanasia and assisted suicide? Will your life be forcefully ended when you get old or become a drain on the Medicare system? Do you care?

I submit that either the right to life belongs to all or it belongs to none. The current laws on abortion therefore are seriously immoral!

Recently, I was on vacation in Florida, and the highlight of a Florida vacation in the winter months is to go to the ocean, lie on the beach, and soak up the warm sun. As I approached the beach, I read a sign that said "If anyone is caught killing a baby sea turtle, they will be fined $10,000.00 or spend 90 days in jail."

How pathetic—sea turtles have protection under state law, and yet an innocent child has no rights or protection to live!

I don't pretend to have all the answers to these moral and deeply painful situations in an unwanted pregnancy, and I cannot explain why God allows terrible things to happen to good people. But I do know that sin is the undeniable truth of evil in our world today!

Today, let us renew our love for life, our sense of responsibility for all human beings, and our determination to protect a child's right to live. Let us work so the laws of our nation may obey the higher law of God.

I could never figure out a recent criminal case that went to court about a man who killed his pregnant wife. He was charged for two counts of murder and found guilty. One count was for his wife and the other was for the murder of the baby in her womb. Can anyone explain this to me? It is a human being when the mother is murdered and her baby also dies but not when it grows inside the mother and it is aborted! How pathetic and warped are our laws!

We all have rights under the constitution, but one of them is not to choose death for another. God is a reality. His creation of life is a reality, and his unconditional love for those he creates is a reality. All else is foolishness. You do not have the right to choose a baby's death!

Don't believe for a moment that mothers are the only ones affected by abortion issues. It is true that mothers carry their baby for nine months within their womb, but conception is not possible without a relationship with a man. Mothers are awesome and great, but so are fathers.

Fathers are an incredible masterpiece of God's plan for salvation because they are the essence of what our Heavenly Father is. An earthly father, out of love and with God's help, can create another life. He loves his children agape style (unconditional). He guides and teaches and wills the best for his sons and daughters, and if necessary, he will even give up his own life to save his children. Of course, these traits of a good father are the working model of our Heavenly Father who also loves, creates, protects, and willingly died for us so that we might live forever.

My friends, it is time for a new perspective on life, time for a new commitment. It is time for a respect-for-creation revolution, which should include every human being at every moment of the day in every place on this earth to stand up for what is right and good in the sight of God and against what is evil and wrong.

It is time to revolt against the vocal minority who are taking away God's rights and destroying the traits of a good father, both earthly and heavenly. It is also time for us to say "enough is enough" and for us to take back our world for our future generations of children.

For the fathers who feel they have made mistakes in raising their children and regret some of their past decisions (know that this includes every father that is and will be), it is time to forget your mistakes. Remember that children do not come with instructions, and you have not had past experience in being a father.

In the future, do everything out of God's love, and with his guidance, the rest will take care of itself.

Be a father to your child as God is to you, and he will help you make the right choices for your son or daughter. Your most important job is to teach them about the God who created them!

And for those fathers who have already raised their children, look forward to the miracle of grandchildren and the chance to love again so intensely that only God could understand. I have always said that if I knew grandchildren were going to be so great, I would have had them first!

Love them, spoil them, and then send them back home to their mother and father to straighten them out again until the next time! For the fathers who are afraid of being a first-time dad, remember that God doesn't make mistakes.

Satan wants you to focus on yourself and the past. Jesus wants you to focus on him and the future.

Love, Pain, or Joy?

If we are to experience life's fullness, we must also experience the trials and pain of life. It is through suffering that we find redemption and truth about who we are. Above every emotion that we are capable of experiencing as a human being, there is one emotion that supersedes all others. We all need to love and be loved. We all need to touch and be touched, and we all need to hold and be held. It is a human condition that makes us complete, and without these emotions, we are incomplete and void of true love.

I don't want to shock you, but are you aware that *love is a four-letter word?*

Many of us, at some time or another in our life, have admired and respected another person enough to call them a walking saint. I believe Mother Teresa of Calcutta, India, was a walking saint, and regardless of our own religious preference, we are blessed to have known a saint in our own lifetime. At this time, she is referred to as Blessed Mother Teresa, and before the book is completed, there is a chance that she will become St. Theresa.

Mother Teresa had dedicated her life to loving and serving the poor and destitute, the poorest of the poor, and she is truly my role model in trying to live my life to the fullest.

I have combined some of her thoughts along with quotes from the founder of the St. Vincent de Paul Society, Frederic Ozanam, to create a powerful combination of words to describe the true meaning of love personified in this remarkable woman's life. Let us hear the voice of God through this holy woman.

Mother Teresa says, "What an honor to visit Jesus Christ." If you could only look at the poor, they will inspire disgust. But when you see Christ in them, you will be attracted and charmed. The poor alone demand your time. Treat them with gentleness, with tenderness, and with love. They are the nobility of heaven.

Picture yourself, millions of souls calling out to you with outstretched arms. So be careful in attending to all of their needs. Do not get angry with them; they have enough to handle with their misfortune. Weep for them. God has made you their consoler. Who will excuse us before God for the loss of so great a number who might have been saved if a little help might have been given to them and a little love had been shown to them?

The greatest disease today is not leprosy or AIDS or tuberculosis, but rather the feeling of being unwanted, uncared for, and deserted by everyone. The greatest evil is the lack of love and the lack of charity, the terrible indifference toward one's neighbor who lives by the roadside, assaulted by exploitation, by corruption, by poverty, and by disease.

In scripture, we hear our Lord telling us to love our neighbor as ourselves. I wonder sometimes if we truly understand God's meaning through these words because so often we distort its intended meaning.

I love pizza. I love that dress. I love my dog. I love to hunt or golf. All of these experiences can use the word *love* to convey a pleasant feeling, but love is so much more than that. The dictionary defines *love* as "a feeling of warm personal attachment or deep affection for another human being and/or object." Though this definition is certainly one that is accepted by most individuals, I do not believe it adequately defines love as God intended it to be, not threefold but one in nature.

A *love-if* relationship is based on a condition that requires one partner to compromise his or her distinct individuality. Usually it consists of the following examples: I will love you *if* you allow me to be the boss of the house. I will love you *if* you allow me one night a week to go out with the guys. This kind of love is always based on a condition, and when that condition is taken away, the love is diminished.

The second kind of love is called *love because*, and it also diminishes the relationship to a condition of reason. I love you *because* you let me be the boss of the household. I love you *because* you let me go out with the guys or girls. This *because* kind of love destroys the true meaning of trust in an unconditional (agape) relationship.

The third love, as I know it, and the love that God intended for us to experience in any relationship, is called *I love you*. Period. It is God's love personified and includes any kind of condition and excludes all conditions. It is agape (unconditional) by its very nature.

No matter what you do, I will love you because I care enough about you to make it unconditional, and I accept who you are—a perfect person with flaws. What a beautiful way to understand love and what it offers to those who accept it. Mother Teresa knew this kind of love!

If you want to experience the same, simply reach out and love the poor!

One day, a vibrant young man and young woman went to a priest and asked him to marry them. They were so much in love and looked forward to spending the rest of their lives together. When asked how much they actually loved each other, the man said, "I would give up my life for this woman as she is everything I ever dreamed of in a spouse." The woman expressed the love for her husband-to-be in the same way, and it seemed they would be the perfect couple.

After this couple was married for seven months, something terrible happened that would challenge their love for each other and change each of their lives forever. The man's wife was in a tragic car accident and broke her neck in two places. The doctor's prognosis was not good, and she ended up in a wheelchair and told she would never walk again.

A month after the accident, the young man went to a priest and asked for an annulment of their marriage. He told the priest that he could not live the rest of his life with a woman who was in a wheelchair and that he was too young to be tied down to this woman twenty-four hours a day. How pathetic but how true the reality of this story hits home for many couples.

He married into a love-if and a love-because kind of marriage, and as soon as the conditions were no longer the same, the marriage dissolved. This conditional love is the same for all relationships and does not pertain to marriage only.

Love is not bought, nor is it earned. It is not acquired by luck or good fortune. Strangely enough, love is the most complex of all human emotions, and it constantly contradicts itself. Perhaps it would make sense to call love an oxymoron because through the intrinsic pleasure of experiencing agape (unconditional) love, we will ultimately experience pain and rejection and frustration as we grasp it.

A famous author once wrote:

> Love anything and your heart may be broken. If you are not willing to risk that, then give your heart to no one! Wrap your love carefully with hobbies, pets, and little luxuries; lock it safe in the coffin of your selfishness and in that coffin, safe, and dark and motionless and airless, it will change; your heart will become unbreakable, impenetrable, irredeemable [and sadly enough, irreparable. It will become a heart empty of any meaning.].

One would ask then, is love worth the risk because the pain can be so severe? The answer is yes, yes, and yes. No human being can be complete without loving another human being and without another human being who returns that love.

And so then, it seems to me that the greatest symbol of love is not just in the heart. Love is far more than just a feeling. It is in the cross, self-giving, self-sacrificing, unconditional, and above all else, it is Christ-given.

First Corinthians13:1–13 explains it best.

> If I speak with the tongues of men and of angels, but do not have love, I have become a noisy gong or a clanging cymbal. If I have the gift of prophesy, and know all mysteries and all knowledge and if I have all faith, so as to remove mountains, but do not have love, I am nothing.
>
> And if I give all my possessions to feed the poor, and if I surrender my body to be burned, but do not have love, it profits me nothing.
>
> Love is patient, love is kind and is not jealous; love does not brag and is not arrogant, does not act unbecomingly; it does not seek its own, is not provoked, does not take into account a wrong suffered, does not rejoice in unrighteousness, but rejoices with the truth; bears all things, believes all things, hopes all things, endures all things.
>
> Love never fails; but if there are gifts of prophecy, they will be done away; if there are tongues, they will cease; if there is knowledge, it will be done away. For we know in part and we prophesy in part; but when the perfect comes, the partial will be done away.
>
> When I was a child, I used to speak like a child, think like a child, reason like a child;

when I became a man; I did away with childish things.

For now we see in a mirror dimly, but then face to face; now I know in part, but then I will know fully just as I also have been fully known. But now faith, hope, love, abide these three; but the greatest of these is love.

We love God only as much as we love our worst enemy.

What Does God Look Like?

I would like to begin this chapter with a question. What is your expectation of God as you struggle with the challenges of life?

The following is an excerpt taken from a book I once read on a daily basis called *God Calling*, and this one particular reflection explains very well the cost of human despair when we do not let go and let God. Read it carefully and you will probably recognize yourself.

> Regret nothing. Not even the sins and failures. When a man views earth's wonders from some mountain height he does not spend his time in dwelling on the stones and stumbles, the faints and failures, that marked his upward path. So with you. Breathe in the rich blessings of each new day—forget all that lies behind you.
>
> Man is so made that he can carry the weight of twenty-four hours, no more. Directly he weighs down with the years behind, and the days ahead, his back breaks. I have promised to help you with the burden of today only, the past I have taken from you and if you, foolish hearts, choose to gather again that burden and bear it, then, indeed, you mock Me to expect Me to share it.

For weal or woe each day is ended. What remains to be lived, the coming twenty-four hours, you must face as you awake.

A man on a march on earth carries only what he needs for that march. Would you pity him if you saw him bearing too the overwhelming weight of the worn-out shoes and uniforms of past marches and years? And yet, in the mental and spiritual life, man does these things. Small wonder My poor world is heartsick and weary.

Not so must *you* act.

Some of the ideas written in this chapter are taken from Pope John Paul II in his exhortation, and though I have incorporated many of my own thoughts with his, I humbly do so with admiration of a holy and great man who is surely destined to sainthood!

Pope John Paul II said,

> Because the lay faithful belong to Christ, Lord and King of the universe, they share in his earthly mission and are called by him to spread that kingdom in history. ... [Therefore], the lay faithful are called to restore to creation all of its original values. ... Bearing fruit is an essential demand of life in Christ and life in the church. ... The person who does not bear fruit does not remain in communion. ... Communion and mission are profoundly connected with each other, they penetrate and imply each other to the point that communion represents both the source and fruit of the mission.

Pope John II is talking about three basic areas of concern that we as Christians should be aware of each day. These areas are the real world, the laity call to evangelize, and the laity response to that call.

Especially in the past fifty years, we have seen a severe breakdown in morality and religious conviction. We have redefined God in our own interpreted image of who we are, and by doing so, we have made a mockery of the likeness and image of the real God. Millions of men, women, and children die each day of poverty and starvation because of political greed and self-interest groups saturated with corruption and deceit and a thinking process of *every man for himself.*

Pope John II says we truly re-crucify Christ when we look at a photograph of a starving child in a third-world country, exhausted and lying on the dirt with flies covering his or her face. We re-crucify Christ when children are abandoned and abused, when teenagers shoot each other in our schools, and when thousands of homeless people live on our city streets, unprotected from the heat and cold and the evil of the emotionally disturbed.

He goes on to say that we crucify Christ when elderly people are alone and forgotten, when infants are born with addictions or HIV, and when people are ravaged by AIDS and cancer.

It is not up to the ordained to evangelize! It is up to you because your numbers are far greater! God sends these forgotten people to us each day, and that means we all have the opportunity to respond to God's will and expectations. It is not enough to be concerned about our own salvation—we must be concerned about everyone we know and meet! Christ asks us to trust as we evangelize his world. We are to plant the seed—he will make it grow.

Let us use the unique, God-given opportunity to evangelize the world so his work might be accomplished and his expectations are met. Only by doing so will our call to holiness and sainthood become a reality. We are all called to be saints, and that is not possible if we don't first believe that God really does exist.

God will hold us if we allow ourselves to become as little children.

Does God Really Exist? Prove It!

For the past two years, I have been involved extensively in our local jail ministry, being challenged from atheists and agnostics alike about the existence of God.

A few weeks ago, an inmate was quite vocal when he told me God wasn't real. He went on to explain that thirty years ago, his father died in a car accident, and if there really was a God, he would have prevented it. He was only ten years old at the time with four brothers and two sisters for his mother to raise alone.

His father's death devastated him and devoured thirty years of peace in his life, causing his alcohol and drug addiction to consume his soul and destroy all that mattered to him as a human being.

The whole class that night joined in discussing his dad's death, trying to make sense of why God allowed these tragedies to happen. I explained that it wasn't God who killed his dad; it was the drunk driver, the car, and the alcohol.

By the end of the evening, he thanked me and said that for the first time in thirty years, he felt peace and understood how wrong he was in blaming God for his dad's death. He assured me that he would start attending church again and allow God to forgive him for such a terrible mistake.

He was released from jail a week later and began to attend church again. This man was young and had no previous history of any serious health problems other than his addiction. A few days after his release, this man died instantly of a heart attack with no apparent history of any heart problems throughout his life.

Thank you, Lord, that he found you before he died!

I know of no person who hasn't at some time doubted the existence of God. When a little child dies at three months old or a spouse dies at the prime of their life, it is easy to question God's existence. God understands that.

St. Thomas Aquinas once said, "God allows evil only so as to make something better result from it." Our question always is, why does God use evil to have a blessing result from it? According to our logic, why not stop evil and not have to use it for blessings or for good?

We can help answer this question by understanding that God is only peace and love and joy, and his ways are always a great mystery to us. We cannot bring God down to our own human level of logic and think we have him figured out. Because God cannot be the originator of something evil, there must be a more logical answer to why evil exists. Does that answer satisfy you? (I didn't think so.)

In violent and painful experiences, evil is being shaped into final perfection. Perhaps it could be described as a physical evil and could include birth defects, hurricanes, tornadoes, floods and mudslides,

Jesus, I Need Your Help

natural catastrophic events, or the miscarriage of a child so desired in the heart of a married couple trying to get pregnant.

On the other hand, moral evil is a result of our own human tendencies. Clearly it includes abortion, pornography, premarital sex and is acted out through our own warped perception of what freedom is. We should never believe there is a God who does evil, but we do need to believe there is a God who allows us to endure life in this world, even when evil shows its ugly face.

In Genesis, creation is described as perfect and holy as were our first parents, Adam and Eve. That perfection is still present in today's world, and therefore, through Jesus's death on a cross and through his resurrection, evil cannot triumph. The worst of all evil is simply a burp to God. In the eternal life and the perfect world to come, evil and suffering will cease to exist.

The most frequently asked question of me in jail is, "Prove to me Deacon Don that God exists." My response is always the same: "I can prove to you there is a God. Can you prove to me there is no God?"

In today's world, it seems that if you believe in God, you are often accused of being mentally ill, delusional, and even irrational. Many say that if you believe in God, you simply don't want to know the truth about life.

Ask yourself these simple questions:

Is it rational or logical to believe in God?

Is there even a logical argument for the existence of God?

Is an atheist mentally ill?

Why do we have something rather than nothing at all?

Why are we here?

Why is the earth here?

Why are there billions upon billions of galaxies and space that cannot be measured?

Why is the sunset so beautiful?

Why do I cry sometimes when I feel great joy?

Who am I that I can take my incredible love for my wife and use that love as one body united, resulting in the creation of a human life?

Finally, who created God? If someone created God, then he would be the real God, not the God we know.

Scientists now claim to have proof of how life and the earth began based on a discovery of a particle so small that the best of microscopes cannot detect it. It is called the *God particle*.

Since we all agree that you cannot get something from nothing, I ask the question, who created the God particle?

Even atheists agree that something cannot come from nothing, so the alternative of reality being self-created must be false.

I read an article from a former atheist who is now a devout Christian, and this is what he said: "I realize that to remain an atheist, I have to believe that nothing produces everything. Those leaps of faith are simply too big for me to accept, especially in light of the absolute and positive case for God's existence."

In other words, the Christian view of a god accounts for the total evidence being much better than an atheistic view. Since belief in atheism can result in loss of eternal life, it would seem that an atheist should be very careful to produce evidence to support his position. They can't, and yet they still do not believe!

My brothers and sisters, if you are struggling with this question, sincerely ask God if he does indeed exist, and he will give you the gift of faith. A gift more precious to you than all the wealth in the world.

We can't love God by memory and prayer alone; we must love by example.

Do you know Jesus's Mother?

I will be telling you about my personal experience with Mary, the Mother of God, in chapter 13, but before you read this chapter, I would now like to tell you about the Mother of God in my own life.

I have come to know Mary in a most intimate way, and she has played a major part in my present-day spiritual journey. To know her is to love her, as the song goes, but this love can only be felt through an understanding of Mary and her place in our church. My prayer for the reader of this book is that you too will come to love our Mother Mary and truly understand the important role she plays in your life and the life of her Son, Jesus. One cannot know Mary without knowing her Son, and one cannot know the Son without knowing his Mother.

Her Son is not a jealous God who feels neglected if one prays and acknowledges his Mother through prayer. In fact, the opposite is true. The more a person loves God, the more that same person loves Mary; and the more that one loves Mary, the more one loves her son. They cannot be separated, nor can they exist without each other. God deemed it this way and desires for us to feel this relationship with his Mother. Is she not the Queen of Peace, the Lady of Truth, the Mother of all creation?

The following story is extremely powerful and will help you understand the role that Mary plays in our everyday life. Please read it carefully and let the Holy Spirit talk to you.

Once there was a rich man who was extremely successful in life. He had all the money he ever needed. He had a beautiful wife, a new car, an expensive home, and thousands of dollars in the bank. God had blessed him with two beautiful and healthy children, and his marriage seemed to be a model for all to follow.

One day, this successful man went to his wife and told her he was leaving and he didn't know for how long, nor did he know where he was going. All he knew was that he was not happy with his life, and something was missing, which caused him to be depressed and unfulfilled.

This man traveled thousands of miles, and he searched the hills and valleys, the cities and little towns, the villages and even other countries, trying to find what was lacking in his life. Days turned into weeks, and weeks turned into months, and months into two years, and still he could not find peace.

Finally, in a little village far away from home, he met a man who told him about a little old lady who might be able to help him find what he was searching for, and she lived high in the mountains above the village. When the rich man asked for her name, he was told it was the *Lady of Truth*.

He climbed this mountain for two days and finally found a cave where he was told this lady lived. As he entered the cave, he found a very old and ugly lady with only one tooth in her mouth and greasy hair that hung down the side of her head, covering her scars and wrinkled face. She smelled like a goat, and as she talked to the rich man, her breath was extremely offensive. He wondered why he had come all this distance to talk to someone like this.

He explained his unhappiness in life, and she listened intently, never taking her eyes off his face and sometimes looking directly into his eyes. She radiated a love that he could not understand. When the man finished talking, he finally understood his unhappiness in life. A peace came over him and filled his heart in a way that he had never experienced before.

As he thanked the lady and started to leave, she asked him to do her a favor. She said, "When you tell everyone about me, please tell them I am young and beautiful." He thought about what this Lady of Truth had asked of him, and it suddenly became very clear what she meant by the words *young* and *beautiful*.

As a young woman, she was like the rich man searching for truth, happiness, and meaning in life. It wasn't until she had searched her whole life, became old and smelly, and had started to wither away that she came to realize she already possessed all of the truth, peace, and beauty in life. She had wasted her entire life looking for something she already had. "Tell everyone I am young and beautiful." She was talking about you and me right now in our life. She was talking about the part of us that keeps searching for what we already have— the truth about life, its meaning, and the knowledge of God, which can only bring the peace that can never be lost.

I suggest that you now stop searching for happiness and the *Lady of Truth*. You have already found her in the person of Mary, the Mother of God.

Let us now begin our journey with Mary by reviewing the basic understanding we have of our Mother and how the church perceives her role in the salvation of souls. We know she was born without original sin, *Immaculate Conception*. We know her husband, Joseph, was chosen as her spouse and provided what was needed for her safety and security. Mary is often referred to as the second Eve, the Queen of Peace, and the Mother of All, born without sin and conceived for the purpose of bringing a savior into the world so that eternal salvation could be given to us through his death.

Mary is the ultimate love personified, and one cannot understand the purpose of life without understanding her reason for existence and her magnificence as a human mother.

Mary is your mother, my mother, and the mother of the church, not just the Catholic Church but every church that exists today. Mary serves one purpose in today's world, and that is to draw people to her Son and eternal salvation. Through all the apparitions over the years, Mary always centers her messages on her Son, Jesus Christ, and asks us to convert, pray, attend daily mass, and fast for the conversion of souls.

Many friends who do not Mary suggest that we worship her, pray to her, and idolize her through statues and prayers. I answer them quickly with the following example: The picture you carry in your wallet of your loved ones doesn't mean you worship them. It simply means you honor them and show the pictures to others as a sign of this love. Catholics do the same through visual statues we have in our churches throughout the world. After all, we relate better by sight because we are a visual people by nature.

We honor our Holy Mother and ask her to lead us to her Son and to intercede on our behalf for conversion and repentance. It seems easier to understand this example if we relate it to our own loving mother during our childhood years. I would always ask my mother for help in changing Dad's mind when he said no to a request to go to the movies or a night out with friends.

Mary simply does the same for us, asking her Son to reconsider our request. Does this mean she has godlike power? Of course not, nor does it even bring attention to her as a powerful force in her Son's life. It simply magnifies her existence as someone special in the eyes of God. Would she not have to be special if she were to be the Mother of God? Would she not understand what it means to carry and give birth to a child, and all the pain and joy that comes with giving birth?

Mary nursed her son and worried about his safety. She cried when he got hurt and kissed his arm when he fell and skinned his elbow. She taught him right from wrong in his childhood days, and as he got older, she could see that she was slowly losing him to the secular and spiritual world in which he was chosen to live and die. It must have been very difficult to see her Son as the chosen one, knowing people were going to hate, betray, and eventually destroy him.

How painful is it to watch the child we bore lay in a hospital dying of cancer or other terminal illnesses? How painful is it to watch or listen to people calling your child a vicious name or displaying hate to its limits? How many parents have to sit on the bleachers when their son is hurt in a football game, wanting to run into the field to be with him, knowing they couldn't for their son's sake and embarrassment.

Mary had it worse than that. She watched her Son die on a cross and couldn't do anything about it because she knew like the injury in the football game that she must not go into the football field! Just a few years ago, my sister-in-law called to tell me her son was in a bad motorcycle accident. She said she wished she could have taken the pain herself. Didn't Mary feel the same way?

It has been said by those who have experienced the death of a child that it is the most painful of all experiences. Those who have lost a child truly understand what these words so inadequately mean. Mary managed to break through the crowd and was walking side by side with her Son. She called to him through the shouting voices. He stopped. Their eyes met, Mary was full of tears of anguish, his full of pain and confusion. Then his eyes said to her, "Courage, Mom, there is a purpose for this" as he tumbled on. Mary knew he was right!

And so we look at Mary through different eyes if we understand her role in the salvation of souls, and we see in a different perspective why her physical appearances through apparitions all over the world are so important for what is surely to come in the distant future.

We are headed down the path of destruction through moral decay and the certain end of family life as God intended it to be. Every great nation since the beginning of time has destroyed itself through greed and moral decay, and the United States is now headed down that path that will destroy its own existence as the greatest nation on earth.

As I said in an earlier chapter, the greatest atrocity ever known to mankind since the beginning of creation is the slaughter of innocent children through abortion. A woman's argument that she has a right over her own body is a personal justification of ending a life that will become an inconvenience in the future. The very core of God's creative nature is to love us enough to create a being in his own image.

I believe most of the tears shed by God and his Mother are tears for the unborn and for those who have decided the fate of human existence personified by what we perceive God's power to be in contrast to our desire to play god. Does this not sound like the story of creation in the garden with Adam and Eve? We play god and pretend we know what is best for ourselves. We even rationalize away the voice of God from within, believing we can be like him if we just grasp the power that God so selfishly holds for himself. Yes, Satan is alive and well!

As Mary stood beneath the cross of her Son, she was destined to stand with all parents who have watched their children and loved ones suffer the sins of the world. She bears the pain of despair and shares the disappointment for those who do not know her Son and his love for all his children. Mary knew that her Son tested the limits of those in control and could see the danger of what was to come.

People were looking for a king, one who could lead the oppressed out of slavery and bring hope to those who lived in despair. Mary could see what hatred was being formulated from the very things her Son taught. Perhaps she was destined to see what was to come so her heart could be filled with the Spirit of her Son and allow her to grasp the moment of what was to be.

Her greatest agony was to watch her Son die on a cross, but perhaps equally as painful was her realization that it was for this reason she was created, and it was for this reason she would become the Mother of all creation. Mary's heart would be pierced many times after the death of her Son. Mary is the Mother of Jesus standing beneath the cross, but she is also our Mother standing with us as we suffer from the moral decay of this world.

A Perfect Institution, Imperfect People

During this time of trial and persecution in the church, it seems that morality and the differences of right and wrong among its members and leaders is at a point of self-destruction. Never in the history of the church have we had so many reasons to rationalize the truth about creation and its Founder. Never have we had more reason to doubt the purpose of our existence in this corrupt and hateful world. People are destroying themselves through greed, hatred, and personal wants and desires.

I remember back forty-eight years ago when I first met my wife, Donna. After the usual courtship and love tactics I used trying to impress this girl I hoped to marry, I told her that if she married me, by the time I was forty-five years old, I would be a millionaire and she would have everything in life she could ever dream of. She told me she didn't want to be married to a millionaire but did want a husband who would love her and be a good father, husband, and provider. I told this silly girl she would have all this, as well as a lot of money and that wealth was important but secondary to my love for her.

Shortly after we were married, we went into business and started to invest in property and rental homes. As the years went by, we had acquired several homes, and through the rental income, we were able to make the payments and continue to buy more real estate until we owned nine homes and some property for future expansion.

I have been told I was a good father as my kids grew up, and I did what I could with my two children—going to their football games and Christmas plays and chaperoning dances—but my thoughts were always on the future and what I could do to earn more money and increase our wealth. One day, I developed stomach trouble. I suspected it was a direct result of stress from too many hours of working. I scheduled an appointment with a doctor friend I had known for many years. He checked me over for ulcers and other illnesses that usually result from stress.

After I was examined, the doctor asked me how I was doing in my life and how much money I was making in the real estate business. As we talked, I explained how many homes I had purchased. He told me that if I kept working as hard as I had been, I would probably make millionaire status by the time I hit forty-five. I was popping the buttons on my shirt as I talked with a man of this stature who recognized a friend who had drive and ambition to become successful in life.

After he finished building me up with his praises and comments about success, he asked me to sit down for a moment as he wanted to tell me something else. He said that if I continued to work as hard as I had been, and if I also continued to maintain the same stress level I had carried over these past years, I would end up a millionaire, but my wife would also end up as a rich widow.

We had plans to build an apartment building that following year, and after hearing what the doctor had said, my wife convinced me to put this project on hold and slow down my life.

This resulted in some changes in my lifestyle, and I did slow down to what I considered a slow man's pace. Our business was very successful; we had accumulated a lot of money in inventory over the years and managed to almost pay off our building and fixtures. Anytime my wife and I wanted to buy a new car or go on a vacation for a week, we would simply draw money out of our savings account and take off for parts unknown for a few days. It was common for us to frequent a restaurant three or four times a week and order whatever we desired, not paying particular attention to the prices.

On February 28, 1982, eight minutes after seven in the evening, something happened that would forever change my life and allow me to understand just how vulnerable and fragile our lives really are. I received a phone call at about seven o' clock in the evening telling me the building next to our store was on fire and that I should come down in case we had some smoke damage. By the time I had arrived at the parking lot at the back of my business, the fire had already spread to the front door and engulfed the entire building in flames. Within thirty minutes, I watched twenty-two years of hard work destroyed by fire, and all the wealth I had accumulated over the years was destroyed.

At the time, this was the most traumatic experience I had ever had in my lifetime, and it seemed like the end of the world as I watched all my possessions burning. I also came to realize how unimportant material wealth is and how fast it can be taken from you. As I look back at my life, I can now say, "Thank you, Lord, for allowing this tragedy to happen to me because it was through this loss that I was able to find myself and establish a new priority in life." When I talk to others about my experience, I am able to understand what God did for me through this fire and teach others the true meaning of life.

It is okay to eat steak and lobster every day of the week if you can afford it, as long as the person next door is not starving to death, and you are ignoring him. It is okay to live in a million-dollar home as long as your neighbor is not living in a cardboard box on the street, and you are not helping him find a home.

God has never condemned wealth as long as it is used for his glory and shared with the less fortunate, downtrodden, and poor of the world. God is love, and he only wants the best in life for all of his creation. We must be careful to never let money replace the importance of God in our life because money and wealth can disappear as fast as we acquire it. Thank you, Lord Jesus, for this beautiful lesson so early in my life.

Holiness is when others say, "If Jesus is like you, then I want to meet Him."

Do people want to meet you?

Who Ministers
to the Minister?

Catchy title to be sure, but do you really understand what a powerful question this is? It is important for us to understand and respect all ministerial vocations, be it priest, bishop, or deacon in the Catholic Church or all pastors in every other denomination. All ministers must and need to receive support and affirmation for their work on a day-to-day basis, especially those who feel threatened by laity.

Many of these threatening feelings are justified since clergy have come from an expected role of doing everything to an individual who is expected to surrender some of the basic jobs expected of them to the nonordained.

Because I am a cleric in the Catholic Church, perhaps I can better describe the emotions and thoughts of the Catholic priest who cannot marry, even though his marriage as a spouse to God and the church is far more rewarding that a human relationship with a specific woman.

Comparing this situation to my own life, I can more easily understand. I have been married to a beautiful woman for forty-eight years. At the saddest and sometimes most difficult times in my life, I have my wife to help me through it. She offers sympathy at times I need it the most and yet holds me accountable for the times I feel sorry for myself and wallow in self-pity.

She is there to comfort me when I am sad and share in my joy when I achieve a goal. I have the important and special gift of sexuality that comes in a loving marriage and have been responsible for helping our Lord create two of the finest sons any man could ever hope for.

When I am lonely, Donna is there for me to talk to; and when I need solitude, she allows me the needed space to think. Above all, growing old together is a special gift of love that cannot be explained. I always believed I knew what real love was, and when I first married my wife, it seemed the feelings I had for her were deep-rooted and never ending. As the years went by, I have learned that love has many levels and intensities that seem to build on one another until its meaning is revealed in God himself.

The first level involved sex as a major consideration in our relationship, and though sex was not the deciding factor for getting married, it certainly played an important role in the relationship. Through the years, this love relationship has grown to include so much more than sex; and even though the intimacy is still an important part of our marriage, it now includes friendship, companionship, and internal relationship of feelings that far exceed the dictionary's definition of *love*.

I'd like to give you a perfect example of what I just described to you. One night after my wife and I had gone to bed, I put my arm around her with my chest against her back and kissed her goodnight. A few minutes later, she said to me, "I love how you make love to me, and I don't always mean sexually." I asked her what she meant since we were both too tired that night for any extra-curricular activity. She went on to explain that sometimes she experiences great sexual pleasure from not having sex but making love as we were at that moment.

You can be sure she had my attention by now, and I again asked her to explain herself. She explained that when I put my arms around her at night and we begin to fall asleep, she feels secure, calm, safe, and very much loved, and that this moment is sometimes as pleasurable as sex itself.

Although I didn't agree this was better than sex, I did understand what she was explaining to me, and I lay awake for over an hour, thinking about her description of love and intimacy in a forty-eight-year-old marriage. I see her as more beautiful today than the day I met her, and I believe that is the real meaning of a lifetime commitment.

Sadly, a priest does not share in many of these most human experiences. A close priest friend once shared his feelings about the priesthood, and several times during our talk, he emphasized the loneliness of his vocation.

More than any other situation, he said the feeling of not having someone to share life with is the most painful of experiences. As I said earlier, sometimes priests are not allowed to be human during times that humanism is the only salvation from despair. Put another way, who ministers to the minister?

I remember one instance a few years ago when I was having a difficult time in my life. I had to make a decision that affected my whole family, and I was not able to sort out the signs that God provided for me. I visited a priest friend at a retreat center and talked for about an hour about the difficult time I was having, and I shared some intimate details about my life. It turned into a very emotional relationship, and by the time we finished, both the priest and I were totally worn out emotionally and physically.

As we walked out of his office, there was a nun who had been waiting for about an hour, and she said it was very important that she talk to him right away. Father told her he was sorry, but he could not meet with her at that moment because he was too worn out emotionally. She insisted again that this was very important, and it wouldn't take much of his time. Father again, with much stronger words, told the nun he could not counsel her at this time, and she would have to come back in a few hours.

It wasn't until after my own ordination and after I had this same experience with others who sought my counsel that I came to realize how draining it is to give yourself in this kind of emotional situation and that the *minister* also needs a break from his role as a caregiver.

Many times I have been guilty of criticizing a priest for what he has or has not done. This reality hit home a few months ago when someone told another person I had made an unkind remark against them while I had actually praised this person. The person confronted me on this accusation, and I could see the pain in her eyes as she told me what another had said. I assured her I had not said anything bad about her, but I could tell the damage had already been done, and she would carry doubt as to my honesty.

This ruined my day, and it took me a long time to get over the hurt and anger I felt for the person who slandered my name. This is a trivial matter compared to the pain a priest feels every time a person criticizes his job performance. One negative comment will tear down the other twenty good comments he heard earlier in the day. We cannot function without affirmation or love, and a priest is no different than the rest of us. In fact, it is conceivable that a priest and/or minister need even more affirmation to help them cope with the stresses of the vocation.

Called the *shepherd of the flock*, he has married the church and taken the vow of celibacy. No different than the vow I took on my wedding day forty-eight years ago to remain faithful and never know another woman intimately. The priest also takes a vow of faithfulness to the Lord and is expected to remain celibate. A priest chooses a marriage to the church in the same way a man chooses to marry a woman, and I do not believe the human factor can excuse or condone an unfaithful act or a breaking of either vow. Every priest I have ever talked to has told me they would choose the celibate life because of God's love.

We have no right to judge another human being, whether he is a priest or any other human being, `td1````````````````````````````````````

but we do have a right to hold another accountable for his immoral actions. I believe a priest is a part of this accountability. Prayer is so critical in this kind of situation.

I have asked many individuals why they feel we have a shortage of priests and ministers in the clerical field, and though many of the ideas varied, there was one answer that stood out from all the rest. In almost all cases, one of the comments was the lack of respect given to clergy. When I asked why they felt the priests did not have the respect of the people, I was told it had to do with the abuse of sexuality.

A week does not pass without a news article about a homosexual priest, a pedophile, or an affair by a clergy. Incidentally, contrary to what many think, the church has less abuse than many other fields where an adult services the needs of children, and that does include some in the teaching vocation.

Why does this happen? What causes a person to break the vows he or she took at the altar, or what causes another human being who has the power of authority to sexually abuse the one over whom they have the power? We can use the excuse "we are human," but certainly that does not condone this type of behavior any more than saying someone else initiated the action.

If the excuse is not the human factor, and I believe it certainly has an influence on this type of sin, then we must believe it goes much deeper in complexity. First, I believe loneliness has a great influence toward unfaithfulness in priests and laity. No person has ever escaped the pain of being alone during a very difficult time, and without having another person to share this pain with, it can become unbearable.

Another example is success and low self-esteem. What good is success if a person does not have someone to share it with? If we cannot look into the mirror and say I love you, we cannot look at others and say we love them. Our own feelings about self have a direct correlation on how we feel about others. If we don't love ourselves, we will fail at maintaining a good moral stance against our own integrity. I have a poster on the wall of my office, and it depicts a little boy looking in the mirror and saying, "God don't make junk."

We are all unique and special in the eyes of Christ, and no one will ever take our place through all eternity. It would seem this uniqueness and oneness in self would be enough to keep us on the road to spiritual gratification and self-fulfillment, but alas, we tend to see the good in others before we see the greatness in ourselves. I believe promiscuity is a direct result of one's self-esteem, and many lives have been destroyed and souls lost through this notion of unworthiness.

Another contributing factor toward sin of the flesh, our spouse, and the church lies in Satan himself. The evil one is sure to visit us during our weakest and most vulnerable times, and it is only through constant awareness of God's presence that we can hope to overcome temptation and evil deeds. Satan is alive and well, and without God's help, it is impossible to overcome sin and moral decay.

Where does this leave us in the battle between right and wrong? Sometimes I wonder if I can ever overcome all the evils and temptations of Satan. Yes, I mean well when I go to confession and tell Christ I will not sin again, but it never seems to work out that way, and little time passes between the confession and the repeat of sin.

Could it be that our Lord understands this dilemma, and the constant falling from his grace fulfills his plan for eternal salvation? I personally believe it does because I know Christ will forgive me as many times as I ask. That forgiveness comes from a sincere repentance and pure heart.

Christ is always *forgiving*; he is the *shepherd* of his people, and he is the *Son of God* and the Alpha Omega of creation. What a satisfying and comforting thought to believe that God knows me more intimately than my own wife and children and loves me even more than life itself. I cannot imagine living in this sometimes evil and frightening world without knowing and trusting my Savior.

Remember this question the next time you criticize the clergy: *who ministers to the minister?*

Personal Experience with Jesus

Over twenty years have passed since my first book was published called *Jesus and Mary: A Journey to Peace*. In that book, I shared my profound and life-changing experience while on a pilgrimage to Medjugorje.

At that time, still fresh in my mind and emotionally charged with the priceless gift that God had given to me, I wrote about miracles and apparitions experienced by several children in the village of Medjugorje in the country of Yugoslavia.

The following account of my experience in Medjugorje is taken word for word from my personal diary and is rewritten to correct its original spelling errors and grammatical inconsistencies recorded upon my return home.

Though I have told this story repeatedly, I really feel the need to tell it again in this book. (God is real, and I know it.)

Having just come back from Medjugorje, Yugoslavia, I find it impossible to put into words what was taking place in this remote little village, and I find it even more difficult to find words that will adequately explain my own personal experience. Upon arriving home from this pilgrimage, I wrote down each experience in a chronological order so nothing would be forgotten as the years go by.

This sharing is my own account of supernatural events that took place in this beautiful little village, and I expect that many who hear this story will experience skepticism and disbelief in what I say, and yet I can only present the facts as they took place. The rest is up to the reader.

Looking back over thirty-two years of being a Catholic convert and at the spiritual growth that has taken place within me over these years, I find it hard to admit that I have always had a difficult time praying to our Blessed Mother. Many times I have tried to understand why I felt guilty while praying the rosary or saying a simple prayer in honor of Mary, and as the years went by, my guilty feelings increased dramatically. I seemed to acknowledge the existence of Mary while apologizing at the same time to Christ for not going directly to him.

As I think how I have struggled with this unnecessary guilt and ignorance of Mary, I wonder how a mature Catholic could allow this to happen. Perhaps my being a Catholic covert was the reason. I knew very little of Mary and even less about how she fit into the spiritual concept of God's existence and plan for the salvation of mankind.

About one year ago, I became interested in the so-called apparitions that were taking place in Medjugorje, Yugoslavia. After reading about the sightings of our Blessed Mother and feeling a calling inside me that I didn't recognize as a call from Christ until after the trip, I was determined to find out for myself if these sightings were in fact real.

Thomas doubted the risen Christ and had to feel the nail holes before he truly believed. I can't help but wonder how I would have reacted to the news that my friend Jesus was alive and well after seeing him die on a cross with my own eyes.

I decided to write for information about a tour that was to take place in July of 1990, and I also mentioned to Father Paul Nomellini, a priest friend and spiritual advisor, that I was thinking of making this pilgrimage. He said he would also like to go and felt a calling in the same strange way as I did.

As the following months went by, the tour of twenty-six people was filled, and we boarded the bus for Chicago and the nonstop flight to Medjugorje. We arrived approximately ten hours after takeoff and suffered some jet lag as we rode the bus through the hills en route to the quaint little biblical village of Medjugorje.

Because there is a seven-hour difference in the time zones, it was almost 3:00AM when we arrived at our lodging, and we took a few hours of nap time. As late morning arrived, we were scheduled to take a bus to the St. James Church located in the center of this little village.

I had read about this beautiful church and how supposedly the apparitions took place in the bell tower located directly in front of the entrance. Needless to say, I was very excited about seeing firsthand where and under what conditions the Mother of Christ would choose to appear to young visionaries.

As we got off the bus, I looked around the church grounds. There were crowds of people rushing into the church, and others were leaving just as fast. My first impression was that Christ would not be very pleased with the fast pace and what seemed to be a lack of reverence to a holy place.

The day ended around 11:00 PM, and we were back in our rooms shortly afterward. Nothing special had taken place throughout the day, and I was quite disappointed in the trip thus far. I had trouble sleeping that night, so I got up and sat outside the room for about an hour. It was a warm evening, and I could hear the crickets chirping and the howling of dogs in the distance.

At that time, I prayed to our Lord and asked him for a sense of peace. I was very disappointed about this little village and its appearance of commercialism, and I asked the Lord to talk to me and explain why I felt so depressed. My words were meaningless, however, and I could not feel any sense of peace or presence of Christ.

We woke the next day about 6:00 AM and quickly had breakfast so we wouldn't miss the bus to St. James Church. We had plans to attend the English mass at 10:00 AM, and when we arrived at the church, people were already leaving from the previous Croatian mass. The mass was inspiring and peaceful, and I felt a little better as I received the body of Christ through the Eucharist.

Even to this day, it bothers me that I didn't recognize what was happening inside me. I guess I was so wrapped up in myself and so full of skepticism and doubt of what was taking place in this village that any communication the Lord wanted to have with me was drowned out by my own disappointment and self-pity.

The problem I had with acknowledging our Blessed Mother, however, was still the same, and I knew I had better resolve it if I was to truly find the peace I sought and understand what Christ expected of me. How does Mary fit into the expectations and teachings of Jesus the Son, and to what extent do I accept her as part of the spiritual journey I was on? I found myself doing what I said I would not do on this trip, and that was to look for the presence of Mary to convince myself that these apparitions were actually real.

I didn't recognize the slow but dramatic change that was taking place within myself because I was too busy looking for signs and miracles such as the spinning sun and rosaries turning to gold. I had told myself that if I was on this pilgrimage to see a vision of Mary or these other miracles I heard so much about, I was truly here for the wrong reason. If I was correct in assuming that Christ had called me to Medjugorje, I knew he wouldn't be very pleased with my response thus far.

Faith should never depend upon miracles or supernatural events. It was later that I came to realize that at the time faith becomes provable, faith no longer becomes necessary. That is the beauty about the gift of faith. It is to be accepted because God tells us to, not because we see!

After I arrived home, I realized it was not a deeper faith I was searching for but rather a deep longing for an intimate relationship with our Blessed Mother, one I had looked for but had never been able to find nor understand.

One of the special privileges this tour offered was a personal visit with the visionaries, and on this particular day, I was able to talk with and ask questions of Ivan. Ivan had been seeing the Blessed Mother since the apparitions started over ten years ago, and his face radiated with a special love that I had never seen before. He was a gentle man, and it was obvious something had touched him profoundly. Truly, his words were not his own, and I felt a peace and excitement during this question-and-answer period.

During the early evening hours, we climbed what is called apparition hill, and when we arrived at the top of this hillside, we found Ivan with his nightly prayer group. They were all gathered together, sitting on the ground and waiting for Mary to appear. Several thousand people were gathered at this site, and we all joined in song and prayer. To experience this event with my wife and priest friend, as well as with hundreds of people of different faiths and backgrounds, was indeed a humbling experience, and I could not absorb nor comprehend all that was taking place at this special moment.

The visionary suddenly dropped to his knees, and his head rose to the night sky. His appearance reminded me of a hypnotic trance, and it actually frightened me a little. The sudden feeling of peace and the overwhelming sense of a holy presence cannot be described in words that could be comprehended. I knew that something profound had taken place, and my eyes searched the trees and sky for just a hint of affirmation. I felt fear and some emotion, and yet I simply could not believe our Blessed Mother could be part of this experience.

After all, we are talking about the *Mother of Christ,* an unnatural state of being in a natural world of logic. This is what I read about in scripture and what my faith has taught me for the past thirty-two years, but experiencing our Holy Mother in this way was beyond the realm of belief. And if the visionary was indeed seeing Mary, it was beyond my comprehension.

It was late when we arrived back at our room, and as I crawled into bed and tried to fall asleep, I could only lay there with my eyes open, thinking about what I had just experienced a few hours earlier. I finally said a prayer to Jesus and openly included Mary as part of that prayer. I asked them both to understand my doubt, and all I asked for during the remaining part of my trip was to understand the relationship he wanted me to have with his Mother. I was convinced this was a holy place and that Christ and Mary were present, but not in the way I would like to believe, that of her physical presence!

It was quite late before I was able to fall asleep, and I wondered if I would be able to get out of bed at four in the morning as scheduled. We were to climb what is called the Mountain of the Cross that morning, and from what I was told, it was a rugged and hazardous climb. My wife and I did wake up in time, and we boarded the bus for a ride to this mountain called Mt. Krizevac.

As we arrived at the bottom of this steep and treacherous mountain, I was not sure if we could make it to the top without an accident. There were many elderly women starting up the trail, some even carrying children, so I figured I should be able to make it to the top if they can, especially wearing my new tennis shoes and hiking equipment.

As we slowly walked the steep trail up the mountain, we came to a rest area about thirty minutes into the climb. At this rest area was one of the fourteen stations of the cross, and Father Paul led us in prayer. It was during this prayer time that I suddenly realized I was called to this mountain for a special purpose.

Tears streamed down my face as I experienced the true presence of a loving and forgiving God. Finally, my heart was starting to open to the reality of where I was. It took about two hours to reach the top of this huge mountain, and though I was exhausted physically, I was emotionally refreshed and excited to see what God had in store for me next.

There in front of me, as I walked off the path we had taken to the top, stood a forty-foot cross, which seemed to reach into the heavens itself, and I stood in awe of its beauty and holiness. How could it be possible to build such a beautiful cross on top of this rugged and rocky mountain? (Later I found out the women of the village had actually carried the cement by hand to the top of this mountain at the request of our Blessed Mother during her first appearance.)

This was a miracle in itself, but far greater was the miracle of where we were. I stood in disbelief as I looked out over the vastness of the land below and the mountains alongside of me. Finally, almost overcome with peace and the feeling that I was standing on holy ground, I walked to the side of the mountain and sat on a rock, gazing at the village below.

I thought of our Lord and how this would be the kind of place he would seek to have uninterrupted prayer with his Father. I can best explain it by saying it was like the doorway to heaven, and I was standing at the front door looking in. It was truly a humbling experience as I sat for about five minutes, mesmerized by the holiness of this mountain and the peace I felt.

I took my sunglasses off to get a better view of the beauty before me, and though I cannot find an explanation for what happened to me next, I suddenly found myself looking directly into the bright sun. Though the sky had no clouds in it, and the sun was so bright that it would have burned my eyes in a few seconds, I could not turn my eyes away from it.

Suddenly, the sun started to pulsate and spin in a fast circular motion, almost like it was out of control, and a round host and sparkling cross appeared in the center. Tears covered my face again as I watched the power of our Lord displayed through this sun. Unknown to me until later that day, Father Paul had experienced the same phenomenon, and we were able to share the experience with each other later.

I had heard of the spinning sun many times from others who had been to Medjugorje, but I never believed that it actually happened. Our Blessed Mother has said in her visits to the visionaries that she would give signs to those who genuinely seek her Son. What a wonderful and precious gift I received that day!

As soon as the spinning stopped, I instantly became aware of a burning in my eyes. Though I had watched the sun for approximately three minutes, it was only seconds after it stopped spinning that I could no longer look at it. Tears once again covered my face as I thought of what had just taken place. I was on an emotional roller coaster, and each moment was another experience greater than the first.

My wife saw my tears and asked me why I was so upset, but I couldn't tell her about the experience at that moment. I needed time to sort everything out and try to put it into some kind of perspective.

By the time we arrived at the bottom of the mountain approximately two hours later, I thought back to what had taken place. The more I thought about the sun spinning, the more I was able to convince myself that what had taken place actually did not take place at all, and it was only my imagination and deep desire to experience a supernatural event that allowed me to think I had seen the sun spinning. My typical doubting Thomas personality had again surfaced and diminished my experience to a mere figment of my imagination.

We arrived back at our room about an hour later, and Donna and I were exhausted. We decided to take a nap before our next visit to St. James Church, which was to be early that evening. It had been a beautiful day, and even the evening gave us temperatures well into the eighties, although we didn't seem to feel the heat as much as the day before.

The rosary began as soon as the visionary arrived, which was usually at six o'clock, and it was led by one of the Franciscans. Outside the church were an estimated two thousand pilgrims, and the inside had standing room only. People were sitting on the floor, as well as standing three deep around the perimeter of the church.

The apparition took place at 6:40 PM, the designated time our Blessed Mother had chosen to meet with the visionaries. At six o'clock, the rosary was recited by all of those attending church, and at exactly 6:40 PM, the church became totally silent, waiting in anticipation of the apparition. The apparition took place in the bell tower directly above the front door of the church, and hundreds of people were looking at their watches in anticipation of Mary's appearance.

I was sitting outside just before the apparition was to take place, and because it was unbearably warm, I told my wife I wanted to go to the side of the church and sit in the shade. She agreed and said she would meet me after the rosary and apparitions were over. I walked to the far end of the church grounds and sat on a flower box directly beneath the shade of a large tree.

As I glanced at my watch, it was almost 6:40 p.m., and I watched in great anticipation for something to indicate the presence of Mary. I looked at the beautiful sky while colors of blue and orange seemed to be reaching into the heavens directly above the mountaintops. I thought how beautiful and calm the earth seemed at that moment, and if Mary were ever to appear, it would seem to be the perfect time.

Suddenly, directly above the bell tower where Mary was to appear, high in the sky and in position with the huge cross we had seen earlier that day, stood the figure of a man clothed in a robe that covered his head and feet. Though I could not believe what I was seeing, I looked directly into the face of Jesus, standing there with his arms outstretched and his eyes looking directly into my face, portraying a gentleness and love that cannot be described.

His outstretched arms moved to a slightly lower position, pointing at the bell tower where his Mother was appearing. In my heart, I heard the words of our Lord as he introduced his Mother to me, and at that very moment, I understood her place in creation. "Behold your Mother, Don, behold your Father, and behold the miracle I place before you."

As soon as the apparition ended, the figure of Christ slowly disappeared, and all I could do is stand in disbelief as I tried to understand what had just taken place. My God, what had just happened to me? Who am I that you would make yourself known to me in this way?

A few minutes later, my wife walked up to me and asked if I was ready to leave and meet our tour group. I looked at her with tears streaming down my face, and I could not speak. I walked away as she kept asking me what was wrong, and I believe she suddenly realized I had to be by myself because she stepped aside as I walked to the edge of the church grounds and started to cry uncontrollably. It took over forty minutes before I could gain my composure, and a peace came over me, and calmness and beauty surrounded me at that moment.

Why would Christ appear to a person like me, one who had just, a few hours earlier, denied the miracle that had taken place on the top of the mountain? Certainly I could understand this happening to Father Paul or Mother Teresa or our pope, but why to a person so unworthy of this priceless gift?

I'm not sure I'll ever find the answer to this question, but I do know this event has changed my life forever. The Lord personally introduced his Mother to me so I could finally find the peace I had searched so long for. Now I understand her love for the world and how she shares in everyone's spiritual journey.

This experience gave me the chance to finally understand and fill the void in my heart that I had tried to fill so many times in the past. The rosary is now a powerful prayer for me, and that is a miracle itself because I did not even know how to say the rosary before Medjugorje.

And so I share this thought with you. If you too are struggling with the rosary and its meaning and purpose in prayer, if you too struggle to understand the concept and scriptural reality of Mary as our Mother and the Queen of Peace, then I tell you with certainty that our Blessed Mother understands and will wait for you to seek her out. At the time your heart is ready to surrender, she will make herself known to you.

My final words are directed to your heart and what you have just heard me tell you. I have not shared this experience so you will think I am someone special and that God has chosen me above others to reveal himself. We are all unique and special to Christ, and he loves all of us in the same capacity, totally unconditionally.

I have not shared so you will believe what I have told you is true and thus bring attention to myself and have others look at me as if I have great importance or that I have been called to be the savior of the world. It doesn't matter if you don't believe my experience. Thomas did not believe in our Lord's resurrection until he felt the nail holes in his hands and feet and was able to talk to him and hear his words of love.

And finally, I did not share this experience so if you are of a different faith than Catholic, you would be converted and want to join the Catholic Church. I am convinced beyond doubt that God does not recognize religion in the way we as humans would like to think. I do not believe anyone should even need this kind of experience to allow his or her faith to grow.

I have shared only so you might understand a little more clearly the place that Mary, our Blessed Mother, plays in our everyday existence; and because you are hearing this from a person who has experienced Christ in this way, it will be a little easier for you to believe.

As Christ watches over us each day and brings comfort and peace during our time of trials and suffering, so does our Mother bring comfort to the troubled soul. She is as real as Christ is real and stands with open arms, ready to protect and love all of those who are willing to cry out her name in love.

Ask Mary for peace and you will receive this peace beyond your imagination. Ask Christ for understanding and you will receive the truth and all the wisdom needed to love him from the depths of your heart. And finally, pray constantly to understand the truth, for the truth alone will set you free.

At the time that faith becomes provable, faith is no longer necessary.

Stories and Poems that Heal the Soul

The following is a collection of stories that I have accumulated over the years, and I have used them many times when I preach the gospel at mass. I wish I could give acknowledgement and credit to the unknown authors for some of these stories, but unfortunately, all of them were given to me by e-mail or under a title of "unknown author." Though I wrote some of these stories myself, I thank the unknown authors for those stories that have touched my life. The inspirational quotes at the end of each chapter of this book are those I learned at an inspiring seminar given by Father Larry Richards, priest and author.

Read them with your heart open to God's spirit and allow your mind to grasp his message of personal and emotional gratification of your own search for peace.

I am sure that regardless of who the authors are for some of these inspirational stories, the words are that of the Holy Spirit speaking through them.

Stories that Heal the Soul

The Presence of Mary and Her Love for a Child

A news article I read years ago told of a five-year-old girl who had been camping with her parents in a state campground, and one day she wandered away from their campsite and wasn't noticed as missing until an hour later. A rescue team was organized, and a search began. The team searched all night and could not find this young child, and as any parent can imagine, the mother and dad were panic-stricken with grief and thinking the worst. There was a fast-moving river only a short distance away from the parents' campsite, and they feared their little girl had fallen into the river and drowned.

Finally, about daybreak, one of the rescue workers noticed a child lying under a log right along the riverbed, and he ran frantically to her. He thought the little girl was dead, and he could barely make himself reach down and pick her up. As he did, she opened her eyes and smiled at the man as if he were someone she knew and trusted. The little girl was alive and well, and she did not cry or even indicate she was afraid after spending the night in the woods alone.

When the child was carried to her camp and her mom and dad saw her, there were tears of joy and relief that God had allowed them to be reunited with their little girl. After a few minutes, the parents asked their daughter if she was afraid of being in the woods alone all night, and the response they received would never be forgotten. The child said, "No, Daddy, I wasn't scared. A nice lady stayed with me all night, and we talked and played games."

Tears flowed down my face as I read this story because it was quite obvious our Blessed Mother had stayed with this little girl that night.

This example is one of many I have heard through the years about the role that Mary plays in our everyday lives, and it seems to me that one cannot hear this kind of story without accepting and believing the reality of our Holy Mother's presence in our world today. That is the reason why life never ends and death never comes.

Our Mother's reality tells us this, and our Lord's words in scripture assure us of this, and the true-life miracles that take place each day verify this. That is why suicide is not possible. One can end his own life through suicide, yet one cannot truly die. Therefore, the problems a person thinks he leaves behind are, in fact, still present. What a wonderful thought to contemplate and how comforting it is to the soul to believe the truth that God gives to us.

Another wonderful reality is that we never die alone, and we will not travel into the new life without someone waiting for us and leading us to the Savior. I remember many examples to prove this statement, but two of them stand out in my mind as quite significant, and I would like to share them with you at this time.

—Unknown Author

My Grandfather's Salvation

My grandfather was eighty-three years old and was in the VA hospital dying of cancer. He spent a total of three months in the hospital, but his last few days were the most meaningful because he experienced a peace at the moment of his death that surpassed all understanding. He had been in a coma for about three weeks, and the doctors had to feed him through a tube to keep him alive. He was not able to talk or even indicate to his visitors and family that he could hear or comprehend what was happening.

One day, late in the afternoon, the family received a call that everyone should come to the hospital as soon as possible as this was grandpa's last moments before death. My mother and father had gone into the room with my grandfather and said they would stay with him until he died, anticipating from the sounds of his breathing that it would only be a few minutes. The death rattle came from deep within my grandfather's chest, and he was filling with fluids rapidly.

Suddenly, he was very quiet, and my parents thought he had just died. A moment of silence passed, and all of a sudden, my grandfather, who only weighed about ninety pounds, did a sit-up in bed and looked toward the window. A smile came to his face that seemed to light up the whole room, and a moment later, he fell back onto the bed and died. What a peaceful smile and what a special gift given to his loved ones as they watched a man being met at the time of his death by our Lord or Blessed Mother. Peace and calm enveloped the room as this man's suffering ended and his new life began.

Angels Are Real

Another beautiful example is about a man dying of cancer, and it was just a matter of hours before his death. His wife went to the hospital this one particular day to stay with him, and she was told that it would only be a few hours before he would die. As she entered his room, she saw her husband sitting up in bed and actually laughing with a man she had never seen before. He introduced this man to her as someone who had just walked into the room to visit with him for a few minutes and that he had brought a lot of comfort to him.

His wife was pleased and thanked the man for taking the time to visit. She noticed her husband's eyes, and they seemed to radiate with a peace she had not seen on his face for many months. Asking her husband why he looked so peaceful, he replied, "Because I know where I am going today, and I am not afraid anymore." After saying these words, he lay back, told his wife he loved her, closed his eyes, and died. The woman turned to the man to thank him again for what he had done, and he was gone, as if he had disappeared into thin air. Since she had been facing the door at the moment of her husband's death, it was impossible for anyone to have left the room without her having seen him leave.

She went to the nurse's station directly outside the door and asked the nurse who this man was and if she had seen him leave. The nurse said she had not seen anyone and that no one could have gotten into the room without her knowledge as she monitored every visitor very carefully in the intensive care unit.

A smile came to the face of this woman even though her spouse had just died as she realized what had just happened. An angel had visited her husband—he was no longer afraid to die. The magnificence of God and his unconditional love for us is his most priceless gift.

—Unknown Author

God Is Always with You

There is a legend about the Cherokee Indian rite of passage into manhood. A father takes his son into the forest, blindfolds him, and leaves him alone. He is required to sit on a stump the whole night and not remove the blindfold until the rays of the morning sun shine through it. He cannot cry out for help to anyone, and he cannot tell the other boys of this experience. Each boy must come into manhood on his own. Once he survives the night, he becomes a man.

The boy is naturally terrified. He can hear all kinds of noises and the wild beasts that are surely around him. Maybe even some human might do him harm. The wind blew the grass and earth and shook his stump, but he sat quietly, knowing that he is forbidden to remove the blindfold. It would be the only way he could become a man!

Finally, after a horrific night, the sun appeared, and the boy removed his blindfold. It was then that he discovered his father sitting on the stump next to him, keeping watch the entire night, protecting his son from harm. We too are never alone, not during our life and clearly not during our death. Even when we don't know it, God is watching over us, sitting on the stump beside us. It is at the moment of our death that our greatest joy is realized.

—Unknown Author

God Will Heal Your Pain

A man who knew he was going to die and wanted to help relieve the pain of his separation for his wife and family wrote the following letter.

His instructions were that this letter was to be read at his funeral, and here is what he had to say:

I know that coping with my death is difficult for all of you. The loss of a loved one is always difficult to accept, and I felt that pending loss as I contemplated my leaving you. God has revealed your pain in the tears that He too is shedding at this time, but I want you to listen to what I have to say, even amid your broken heart and ocean of tears.

This heaven is a place that stretches the imagination. It cannot be described, nor has it ever been experienced during the time I spent on earth, even among our best years of young love and our understanding of oneness in old age.

It is so strange what God has designed for us after we leave earth's dwelling and depart from those whom we love so much.

I am able to remember the infinite pleasure of our young love, fumbling through our awkwardness of love making to the true experience of making love, and I am filled with awesome memories of becoming one in body and spirit.

I am able to remember our years of struggle and the uncertainty of what the future held for us at such a young age, and I am able to envision the thoughts of immortality which told us both that we would never get old. Even if we did, it would not matter because our love would sustain us in caring for one another.

I am able to remember the unbelievable joy from the birth of our children and grandchildren and their oneness in love with each other, the greatest gift a child can give to a parent.

I always thought that heaven was only a place of tranquility, void of all memory of the past and where nothing could distract the soul from the beauty of God's presence. Now I know that it is so much more than that. God has transformed the soul into a vessel of memories that sustains the separation with a sense of what is yet to come.

If you really love me, then I ask you to hear what I have to say. Do not be afraid any longer. Do not allow yourself to grieve over what is not lost. Do not despair from my death but rather rejoice over what is to be. God has a plan that includes you in my death! He has arranged that someday soon we will be side by side again, smelling the freshness of the flowers and gazing upon the beauty of their colors while running through the fields and forests with smells of nature and a world that is to be forever unchanged.

I know this because I am experiencing God's fullness of life through His love for me. I know because I have the memories of the life behind and the knowledge of the life ahead. And I know because God's gentle eyes are telling me so at this moment.

Grasp the fullness of life and every moment God gives you while on earth and know that this reality continues after death, a reality we will again share together.

A Love Made Perfect

Our faith teaches that God has created us in his own image, and in order for perfection to be present in this creation, God introduced love into the world.

This is not an ordinary love that can be improved by human desire, but rather a love, divine in nature, created in heaven and inspired by the Holy Spirit. A love made perfect, but only perfect in the eyes of God who knows beyond human imagination.

If we accept this perfect love, we must also accept its consequences, for surely a perfect love will eventually lead to a temporary suffering.

For every one of us, death will someday become part of life, and we will experience the pain of separation from those we love. We will even doubt the existence of God occasionally, but we still go on with life, searching for the purpose of suffering. Ultimately, we will reach a moment of surrender and let go of the pain and start again. That is what life is about, and that is what allows us to be fully human and fully alive. Through it all, the conclusion is the same. God always replaces suffering with joy.

Life is for the living, and it is to be treasured as a priceless gift from God. We are to live each moment as if it were our last and grasp every opportunity to love again because it is a human need to love and be loved.

A Woman in Disguise

I was waiting for the taxi to pick me up and drive me back to the hotel. I was seated on the wood bench adjacent to but across from the quaint little restaurant in which I had just eaten a large steak dinner. As I looked around, kind of people watching, I noticed a little girl about seven years of age standing outside the small open restaurant and gazing through the window, which separated the inside of the restaurant from the patio deck and the people outside the restaurant.

All of them were eating and drinking an abundance of food and wine, and their laughter carried a weird tone of self-indulgence and an indifference to the other poor who walked past this little girl with heads hung low and faces void of any joy. I found out later that it had been yesterday since her last meal, and her little belly hurt a lot. As she watched the rich people eating, she wondered why God didn't love her like he did the others who always had plenty of food each day.

Perhaps it hurt her even more and made it even more difficult to understand when she saw the people get up from the table and leave a lot of the food lay there, only to be disposed of in the garbage later on. Her precious little smile, among the tears that flowed down her face, silently told me that she was lost, scared, defeated, and ashamed of her existence, and she wished that God would love her too.

I knew I had a little time before the taxi would arrive, so I decided to cross the street and ask this little child what she was doing on the streets by herself at such a young age.

When I approached her, she shied back a little and looked at me with a hint of fear and a childlike trust that most little girls would be afraid to extend to a stranger. I asked her what she was doing on the streets alone, and she just smiled and extended her hand and little basket toward me.

It was at that moment that I saw a small handful of flowers, already wilted from the heat of the sun yet still presentable to sell to anyone who would notice her looking up at them with her incredibly beautiful black eyes and long silky hair. It became obvious to me that this little girl was selling flowers to earn a little money, and she was almost at the end of the day. The day had not been a very good one for sales.

I asked her how much they were, and her face lit up with a smile as big as the Hoover Dam. She told me that I could have one rose for one dollar or two roses for one dollar and fifty cents. After looking over the selection, I asked her if she would consider selling all of them for one hundred dollars, and she just looked at me like I was the craziest man she had ever met!

She handed the flowers to me, and I placed a hundred-dollar bill into her hands. I told her to hide the money in her pockets so that no one would know she had that amount of money in her possession.

When I stepped back a little to look into her face, she wrapped her arms around me and cried a bucket of tears. I felt a little uncomfortable as this precious little child clung to me and continued her tears. I knew that this little girl had just received almost six months worth of income in this one transaction, and she could not believe that this was really happening.

After she let go of my hand, I asked her if she would like to have a little to eat because I had decided to stay a few more hours and was hoping she would keep me company. She looked up at me and said she was very hungry and would surely like to eat something, but she was told people like her were not allowed in this restaurant. I told her she was allowed to go into the restaurant as long as she was with me, and I would be very proud to have her as my date!

"After you're done eating, let's have an ice cream sundae for dessert," I said as we entered the restaurant.

"I really like ice cream," she said. "But I haven't had any for a long, long time because my family is very poor."

It was hard to imagine any little girl eating that much food, but I saw it for myself!

After she was finished, I told the waiter to bring me the largest sundae he could make, and the little girl's eyes almost popped out of her head as they placed it in front of her. Chocolate, whipped cream, bananas, strawberries, pineapples, and a sprinkle of peanuts made this ice cream sundae a true work of art. (A half hour later, she finished her last spoonful and sat back in the chair looking like she was going to burst at the seams.)

I paid the bill. We walked outside, and I told her I had to leave now and that I really wished her well. The only words I heard were "thank you, sir!"

As she stood on the street watching me walk away, I yelled back to her, "I forgot to ask you your name, little girl!"

She smiled at me and said, "Mary."

"That's a nice name!" I yelled back, and my taxi drove up at that moment.

As I got into the cab, I looked toward Mary to say my last good-bye. Mary was not there, but standing in her spot was a beautiful adult woman clothed in a blue and white robe, covering her feet and radiating a glow of light over her head. I have never gazed upon a woman more beautiful and radiant, and I knew that something special had just happened to me though I could not believe my eyes!

The Lady's voice said to me, "My Son knows what you just did, and he is very proud of you!"

Slowly she disappeared from sight, and the street was empty of all the poor who were congregated together just a few minutes before.

When I arrived back at my hotel, I reached into my pocket to pay the cab driver, and there in my pocket was the hundred-dollar bill I had given to little Mary. I handed the cab fare to the driver, and he asked me if I was okay as the tears streamed down my face. I told him I had never been better!

A Ragged Old Man

We were the only family with children in the restaurant. I sat my two-year-old Nicole in a high chair and noticed everyone was quietly sitting and talking. Suddenly, Nicole squealed with glee and said hi. She pounded her fat baby hands on the high-chair tray. Her eyes were crinkled in laughter, and her mouth was bared in a toothless grin as she wriggled and giggled with merriment.

I looked around and saw the source of her merriment. It was a man whose pants were baggy, and his toes poked out of would-be shoes. His shirt was dirty, and his hair was uncombed and unwashed. His whiskers were too short to be called a beard, and his nose was so varicose it looked like a road map. We were too far from him to smell, but I was sure he smelled. His hands waved and flapped on loose wrists.

"Hi there, baby, hi there, big girl. I see you, sweetie," the man said to my daughter.

My husband and I exchanged looks. What do we do now?

Nicole continued to laugh and answer hi. Everyone in the restaurant noticed and looked at us and then at the man. The old man was creating a nuisance with my beautiful baby. Our meal came, and the man began shouting from across the room, "Do ya patty-cake? Do you know peekaboo? Hey, look, she knows peekaboo."

Nobody thought the old man was cute. He was obviously drunk. My husband and I were embarrassed. We ate in silence, all except for Nicole who was enjoying and admiring the skid-row bum who in turn reciprocated her cute comments.

We finally got through the meal and headed for the door. My husband went to pay the check and told me to meet him at the parking lot. The old man sat poised between the door and me. "Lord, just let me out of here before he speaks to me or Nicole," I prayed. As I drew closer to the man, I turned my back trying to sidestep him and avoid any air he might be breathing.

As I did, Nicole leaned over my arm, reaching with both arms in a baby's pick-me-up position. Before I could stop him, Nicole had propelled herself from my arms to the man.

Suddenly, a very old smelly man and a very young baby consummated their love and kinship. Nicole, in an act of total trust, love, and submission laid her tiny head upon the man's ragged shoulder. The man's eyes closed, and I saw tears cover his face.

His aged hands full of grime, pain, and hard labor cradled my baby's bottom and stroked her back. No two beings have ever loved so deeply for so short a time.

I stood awestruck. The old man rocked and cradled Nicole in his arms, and his eyes opened and set squarely on mine. He said in a firm commanding voice, "You take care of this baby." Somehow, I managed "I will" from a throat that contained a stone.

He pried Nicole from his chest lovingly and longingly as though he were in pain. I received my baby, and the man said, "God bless you, ma'am. I lost my little girl and my wife in a car accident last year, and I haven't been able to get myself together since that day. Then I lost my job and my home! To hold a little child like this again has been the greatest Christmas gift I have ever received, especially since I lost my daughter and wife. God bless you!"

I said nothing more than a muttered thanks. With Nicole in my arms, I ran for the car. My husband was wondering why I was crying and holding our daughter so tightly and why I was saying, "'My God, my God, forgive me."

I had just witnessed Christ's love shown through the innocence of a tiny child who saw no sin, who made no judgment, a child who saw a soul and a mother who saw a suit of clothes. I was a Christian who was blind, holding a child who was not. I felt it was God asking if I was willing to share my daughter for a moment when he shared his for all eternity. How did God feel when he put his baby in our arms two thousand years ago?

The ragged old man unwittingly had reminded me that to enter the kingdom of God, we must first become as little children.

—Unknown Author

Carl the Waterman

Carl was a quiet man. He didn't talk much. He would always greet you with a big smile and a firm handshake. Even after living in our neighborhood for over fifty years, no one could really say they knew him very well. Before his retirement, he took the bus to work each morning. The lone sight of him walking down the street often worried us. He had a slight limp from a bullet wound received in WWII.

Watching him, we worried that although he had survived WWII, he may not make it through our changing uptown neighborhood with its ever-increasing random violence, gangs, and drug activity.

When he saw the flyer at our local church asking for volunteers for caring for the gardens behind the minister's residence, he responded in his characteristically unassuming manner. Without fanfare, he just signed up.

He was well into his eighty-seventh year when the very thing we had always feared finally happened. He was just finishing his watering for the day when three gang members approached him. Ignoring their attempt to intimidate him, he simply asked, "Would you like a drink from the hose?"

The tallest and toughest-looking of the three said, "Yeah, sure" with a malevolent little smile. As Carl offered the hose to him, the other two grabbed Carl's arm, throwing him down.

As the hose snaked crazily over the ground, dousing everything in its way, Carl's assailants stole his retirement watch and his wallet and then fled.

Carl tried to get himself up, but he had been thrown down on his bad leg. He lay there trying to gather himself as the minister came running to help him. Although the minister had witnessed the attack from his window, he couldn't get there fast enough to stop it.

"Carl, are you okay? Are you hurt?" the minister kept asking as he helped Carl to his feet.

Carl just passed a hand over his brow and sighed, shaking his head. "Just some punk kids. I hope they'll wise up someday." His wet clothes clung to his slight frame as he bent to pick up the hose. He adjusted the nozzle again and started to water.

Confused and a little concerned, the minister asked, "Carl, what are you doing?"

"I've got to finish my watering. It's been very dry lately," came the calm reply.

Satisfying himself that Carl really was all right, the minister could only marvel. Carl was a man from a different time and place.

A few weeks later, the three returned. Just as before, their threat was unchallenged. Carl again offered them a drink from his hose. This time they didn't rob him. They wrenched the hose from his hand and drenched him head to foot in the icy water. When they had finished their humiliation of him, they sauntered off down the street, throwing catcalls and curses, falling over one another, and laughing at the hilarity of what they had just done.

Carl just watched them. Then he turned toward the warmth-giving sun, picked up his hose, and went on with his watering.

The summer was quickly fading into fall. Carl was doing some tilling when he was startled by the sudden approach of someone behind him. He stumbled and fell into some evergreen branches. As he struggled to regain his footing, he turned to see the tall leader of his summer tormentors reaching down for him. He braced himself for the expected attack.

"Don't worry, old man, I'm not going to hurt you this time," the young man spoke softly, still offering the tattooed and scarred hand to

Carl. As he helped Carl get up, the man pulled a crumpled bag from his pocket and handed it to Carl.

"What's this?" Carl asked.

"It's your stuff," the man explained. "It's your stuff back. Even the money in your wallet."

"I don't understand," Carl said. "Why would you help me now?"

The man shifted his feet, seeming embarrassed and ill at ease. "I learned something from you," he said. "I ran with that gang and hurt people like you. We picked you because you were old, and we knew we could do it. But every time we came and did something to you, instead of yelling and fighting back, you tried to give us a drink. You didn't hate us for hating you. You kept showing love against our hate."

He stopped for a moment. "I couldn't sleep after we stole your stuff, so here it is back." He paused for another awkward moment, not knowing what more there was to say. "That bag's my way of saying thanks for straightening me out, I guess." And with that, he walked off down the street.

Carl looked down at the sack in his hands and gingerly opened it. He took out his retirement watch and put it back on his wrist. Opening his wallet, he checked for his wedding photo. He gazed for a moment at the young bride who still smiled back at him from all those years ago.

Carl died one cold day after Christmas that winter. Many people attended his funeral in spite of the weather. In particular, the minister noticed a tall young man whom he didn't know sitting quietly in a distant corner of the church.

The minister spoke of Carl's garden as a lesson in life. In a voice made thick with unshed tears, he said, "Do your best and make your garden as beautiful as you can. We will never forget Carl and his garden."

The following spring, another flyer went up. It read: "Person needed to care for Carl's garden." The flyer went unnoticed by the busy parishioners until one day a knock was heard at the minister's office door. Opening the door, the minister saw a pair of scarred and tattooed hands holding the flyer. "I believe this is my job, if you'll have me," the young man said.

The minister recognized him as the same young man who had returned the stolen watch and wallet to Carl. He knew that Carl's kindness had turned this man's life around.

As the minister handed him the keys to the garden shed, he said, "Yes, go take care of Carl's garden and honor him."

The man went to work, and over the next several years, he tended the flowers and vegetables just as Carl had done. During that time, he went to college, got married, and became a prominent member of the community. But he never forgot his promise to Carl's memory and kept the garden as beautiful as he thought Carl would have kept it.

One day, he approached the new minister and told him that he couldn't care for the garden any longer. He explained with a shy and happy smile, "My wife just had a baby boy last night, and she's bringing him home on Saturday."

"Well, congratulations!" said the minister as he was handed the garden shed keys. "That's wonderful! What's the baby's name?"

"Carl," he replied.

—Unknown Author

God Has a Sense of Humor

During World War II, a US marine was separated from his unit on a Pacific island. The fighting had been intense, and in the smoke and the crossfire, he had lost touch with his comrades. Alone in the jungle, he could hear enemy soldiers coming in his direction.

Scrambling for cover, he found his way up a high ridge to several small caves in the rock. Quickly he crawled inside one of the caves. Although safe for the moment, he realized that once the enemy soldiers looking for him swept up the ridge, they would quickly search all the caves and he would be killed.

As he waited, he prayed, "Lord, if it be your will, please protect me. Whatever your will though, I love you and trust you. Amen." After praying, he lay quietly listening to the enemy begin to draw close. He thought, *Well, I guess the Lord isn't going to help me out of this one.* Then he saw a spider begin to build a web over the front of his cave.

As he watched listening to the enemy searching for him all the while, the spider layered strand after strand of web across the opening of the cave. *Hah*, he thought. *What I need is a brick wall and what the Lord has sent me is a spiderweb. God does have a sense of humor.*

As the enemy drew closer, he watched from the darkness of his hideout and could see them searching one cave after another. As they came to his, he got ready to make his last stand. To his amazement, however, after glancing in the direction of his cave, they moved on. Suddenly, he realized that with the spiderweb over the entrance, his cave looked as if no one had entered it for quite a while.

"Lord, forgive me," prayed the young man. "I had forgotten that in you, a spider's web is stronger than a brick wall."

—Unknown Author

Earthly Angels Pay a Visit

It was Christmas Eve 1949. I was fifteen and feeling sad because there was not enough money to buy me the dress that I wanted. We did the chores early that night, so I figured Pa wanted a little extra time for us to read the Bible.

After supper, I took off my boots, stretched out by the fireplace, and waited for Pa to start reading. I was still feeling sorry for myself and, to be honest, wasn't in much of a mood to read scriptures. But Pa didn't get the Bible; instead, he bundled up again and went outside. I couldn't figure it out because we had already done all the chores.

It was a cold clear night, and the ice was in Pa's beard when he came back in. "Come on, Elizabeth," he said. "Bundle up. It's cold out."

I was upset. Not only wasn't I getting the dress, now Pa was dragging me out in the cold. I put on my coat and boots, and Ma gave me a mysterious smile as I opened the door. Something was up.

Outside, I became even more dismayed. There, in front of the house, was the work team, already hitched to the big sled. Whatever we were going to do wasn't going to be a quick job. I reluctantly climbed beside Pa, the cold already biting me. We pulled in front of the woodshed, put on the high sideboards and started loading wood—the wood we spent all summer hauling down from the mountain and all fall sawing into blocks and splitting.

Finally, I asked, "Pa, what are you doing?"

"You been by the widow Clark's lately?" he asked. (Mrs. Clark lived about two miles down the road. Her husband had died a year before and left her with three children.)

"Yeah," I said. "Why?"

"I rode by just today," Pa said. "Little Jake was out digging around in the woodpile trying to find a few chips. They're out of wood, Elizabeth."

That was all he said, and we loaded the sled so high that I began to wonder if the horses would be able to pull it. Pa then went to the smokehouse and took down a big ham and a side of bacon, telling me to go load them. He returned to the sled carrying a sack of flour over his right shoulder and a smaller sack of something in his left hand.

"What's in the sack?" I asked.

"Shoes. They're out of shoes. Little Jake had gunnysacks wrapped around his feet when he was out in the woodpile. I got the children a little candy too. It just wouldn't be Christmas without candy."

We rode the two miles to the Clarks' place in silence. I tried to think through what Pa was doing. We did have a big woodpile, meat, and flour, so we could spare that, but I knew we didn't have any money. Widow Clark had closer neighbors than we did; it shouldn't have been our concern.

We unloaded the wood and went to the door. We knocked. The door opened a crack, and a timid voice said, "Who is it?"

"James Cotton, ma'am, and my daughter, Elizabeth. Could we come in for a bit?"

Mrs. Clark opened the door and let us in. She had a blanket wrapped around her shoulders. The children were huddled beneath another blanket, sitting in front of a small fire in the fireplace. Widow Clark fumbled with a match and lit the lamp.

"We brought you a few things, ma'am," Pa said and set the sack of flour and meat on the table. Pa handed her the other sack. She opened it hesitatingly and took out the shoes, one pair at a time. There was a pair for her and one for each of the children—sturdy shoes that would last.

She bit her lower lip to keep it from trembling as tears filled her eyes and ran down her cheeks. She looked at Pa as if she wanted to say something, but it wouldn't come out.

"We brought a load of wood too, ma'am," Pa said. He turned to me and said, "Elizabeth, go bring in enough to last awhile. Let's get that fire roaring and heat this place up."

I wasn't the same person when I went to bring in the wood. I had a big lump in my throat and tears in my eyes.

We soon had the fire blazing, and everyone's spirits soared. The kids giggled when Pa handed them each a piece of candy, and Widow Clark looked on with a smile that probably hadn't crossed her face for a long time. "God bless you," she said. "I know the Lord sent you. The children and I prayed that he would send one of his angels to spare us."

Pa insisted that everyone try on the shoes before we left. I was amazed when they all fit, and I wondered how he had known what sizes to get. Then I guessed that if he was on an errand for the Lord, the Lord made sure he got things right. Pa took each of the kids in his big arms and gave them a hug. They clung to him and didn't want us to go. I could see that they missed their Pa and was glad that I still had mine.

At the door, Pa turned to Widow Clark and said, "The missus wanted me to invite you and the children over for Christmas dinner tomorrow. The turkey will be more than the three of us can eat, and a man can get cantankerous if he has to eat turkey for too many meals. We'll be by to get you about eleven. It'll be nice to have some little ones around again."

Mrs. Clark nodded and said, "Thank you, Brother Cotton. I don't have to say, 'May the Lord bless.' I know for certain that he will."

On the sled, after we had gone away, Pa turned to me and explained that he and Ma had tucked away money here and there all year for my dress. Yesterday, on the way to town, he had seen little Jake with his feet wrapped in gunnysacks. "I knew what I had to do," he said. "I spent the money for shoes and a little candy for those children. I hope you understand."

I understood very well, and I was glad Pa had done it. My father had given me a lot more than a dress. He had given me the look on Widow Clark's face, the smiles of her children, and the best Christmas memory of my life.

—Unknown Author

Gramma's Precious Hands

Grandma, some ninety plus years, sat feebly on the patio bench. She didn't move, just sat with her head down staring at her hands. When I sat down beside her, she didn't acknowledge my presence; and the longer I sat, the more I wondered if she was okay.

Finally, not really wanting to disturb her but wanting to check on her at the same time, I asked her if she was okay. She raised her head, looked at me, and smiled. "Yes, I'm fine, thank you for asking," she said in a clear, strong voice.

"I didn't mean to disturb you, Grandma, but you were just sitting here staring at your hands, and I wanted to make sure you were okay," I explained to her.

"Have you ever looked at your hands?" she asked. "I mean really looked at your hands?"

I slowly opened my hands and stared down at them. I turned them over, palms up and then palms down. No, I guess I had never really looked at my hands as I tried to figure out the point she was making. Grandma smiled and told me the following story:

Stop and think for a moment about the hands you have, how they have served you so well throughout your years. These hands, though wrinkled, shriveled, and weak have been the tools I have used all my life to reach out and grab and embrace life. They braced and caught my fall when as a toddler I crashed upon the floor.

They put food in my mouth and clothes on my back. As a child, my mother taught me to fold them in prayer. They tied my shoes and pulled on my boots. They held my husband and wiped my tears when he went off to war. They have been dirty, scraped and raw, swollen and bent!

They were uneasy and clumsy when I tried to hold my newborn son. Decorated with my wedding band, they showed the world that I was married and loved someone special.

They wrote my letters to him and trembled and shook when I buried my parents and spouse. They have held my children and grandchildren, consoled neighbors, and shook in fists of anger when I didn't understand. They have covered my face, combed my hair, and washed and cleansed the rest of my body.

They have been sticky and wet, bent and broken, dried and raw. And to this day, when not much of anything else of me works really well, these hands hold me up, lay me down, and again continue to fold in prayer.

These hands are the mark of where I've been and the ruggedness of life. But more importantly, it will be these hands that God will reach out and take when he leads me home. And with my hands, he will lift me to his side, and there I will use these hands to touch the face of Christ.

I will never look at my hands the same again. God reached out and took my grandma's hands and led her home the next night. When my hands are hurt or sore or when I stroke the face of my children and husband, I think of Grandma. I know the hands of God have held her, and I too want to touch the face of God and feel his hands upon me.

—Unknown Author

Now That's God

It was one of the hottest days of the dry season. We had not seen rain in almost a month. The crops were dying, cows had stopped giving milk, and the creeks and streams were long gone back into the earth. It was a dry season that would bankrupt several farmers before it was through.

Every day, my husband and his brothers would go about the arduous process of trying to get water to the fields. Lately this process had involved taking a truck to the local water-rendering plant and filling it up with water, but severe rationing had cut everyone off. If we didn't see some rain soon—we would lose everything.

It was on this day that I learned the true lesson of sharing and witnessed the only miracle I have seen with my own eyes. I was in the kitchen making lunch for my husband and his brothers when I saw my six-year-old son, Billy, walking toward the woods. He wasn't walking with the usual carefree abandon of a youth but with a serious purpose. I could only see his back. He was obviously walking with great effort, trying to be as still as possible.

Minutes after he disappeared into the woods, he came running out again toward the house. I went back to making sandwiches, thinking that whatever task he had been doing was completed. Moments later, however, he was once again walking in that slow, purposeful stride toward the woods. This activity went on for an hour, walking carefully to the woods then running back to the house.

Finally I couldn't take it any longer and crept out of the house and followed him on his journey (being very careful not to be seen as he was obviously doing important work and didn't need his mommy checking up on him). He was cupping both hands in front of him as he walked, being very careful not to spill the water he held in them, maybe two or three tablespoons were held in his tiny hands.

I sneaked close as he went into the woods. Branches and thorns slapped his little face, but he did not try to avoid them. He had a much higher purpose. As I leaned in to spy on him, I saw the most amazing sight.

Several large deer loomed in front of him. Billy walked right up to them. I almost screamed for him to get away. A huge buck with elaborate antlers was dangerously close, but the buck did not threaten him. He didn't even move as Billy knelt down. And I saw a tiny fawn lying on the ground, obviously suffering from dehydration and heat exhaustion, lift its head with great effort to lap up the water cupped in my beautiful boy's hand. When the water was gone, Billy jumped up to run back to the house, and I hid behind a tree.

I followed him back to the house to a spigot to which we had shut off the water. Billy opened it all the way up, and a small trickle began to creep out. He knelt there, letting the drip, drip slowly fill up his makeshift cup as the sun beat down on his little back.

And it came clear to me: the trouble he had gotten into for playing with the hose the week before, the lecture he had received about the importance of not wasting water, the reason he didn't ask me to help him. It took almost twenty minutes for the drops to fill his hands. When he stood up and began the trek back, I was there in front of him.

His little eyes just filled with tears. "I'm not wasting" was all he said. As he began his walk, I joined him with a small pot of water from the kitchen. I let him tend to the fawn. I stayed away. It was his job. I stood on the edge of the woods watching the most beautiful heart I have ever known, working so hard to save another life.

As the tears that rolled down my face began to hit the ground, other drops—and more drops—and more suddenly joined them. I looked up at the sky. It was as if God himself was weeping with pride.

Some will probably say that this was all just a huge coincidence. Those miracles don't really exist, that it was bound to rain sometime. And I can't argue with that. I'm not going to try. All I can say is that the rain that came that day saved our farm, just like the actions of one little boy saved another.

I don't know if anyone will believe this, but it's a true story. I just had to send it out to honor the memory of my beautiful Billy, who died a short time after this incident. He was taken from me much too soon, but not before showing me the true face of God in a little sunburned body. (No one can make it in life without God, and my son, Billie, taught me that.)

—Unknown Author

Saved on Highway 109

They said a drunken man in an Oldsmobile had run the light that caused the six-car pileup on Highway 109 that night. When broken bodies lay about and blood was everywhere, the sirens screamed out eulogies, for death was in the air.

A mother, trapped inside her car, was heard above the noise, her plaintive plea nearly split the air, "Oh God, please spare my boys!" She fought to loose her pinned hands. She struggled to get free, but mangled metal held her fast in grim captivity.

Her frightened eyes then focused on where the backseat once had been, but all she saw was broken glass and two children's seats crushed in. Her twins were nowhere to be seen. She did not hear them cry, and then she prayed they'd been thrown free, "Oh God, please don't let them die!"

Then firemen came and cut her loose. When they searched the back, they found no little boys, but the seatbelts were intact. They thought the woman had gone mad and was traveling alone, but when they turned to question her, they discovered she was gone.

Policemen saw her running wild and screaming above the noise in beseeching supplication, "Please, God, help me find my boys! They're four years old and wear blue shirts, their jeans are blue to match."

One cop spoke up, "They're in my car, and they don't have a scratch. They said their daddy put them there and gave them each a cone then told them both to wait for Mom to come and take them home. I've searched the area high and low, but I can't find their dad. He must have fled the scene, I guess, and that is very bad."

The mother hugged the twins and said while wiping away her tears, "He could not have fled the scene…he's been dead for over a year."

The cop just looked confused and asked, "Now how can that be true?" He heard the boys say, "Mommy, Daddy came and left a kiss for you. He told us not to worry and that you would be all right, and then he put us in this car with the pretty, flashing lights We wanted him to stay with us because we miss him so, but Mommy, he just hugged us tight and said he had to go. He said someday we'd understand and he told us not to fuss, and he said to tell you, Mommy, he's watching over us."

The mother knew without a doubt that what they spoke was true, for she recalled their dad's last words, "I will watch over you." The firemen's notes could not explain the twisted, mangled car and how the three of them escaped without a single scar, but on the cop's report was written in print so very fine, "An angel walked the beat tonight on Highway 109."

—Unknown Author

God Lives Under the Bed

I envy Kevin. My brother, Kevin, thinks God lives under his bed. At least that's what I heard him say one night. He was praying out loud in his dark bedroom, and I stopped to listen, "Are you there, God?" he said. "Where are you? Oh, I see. Under the bed…"

I giggled softly and tiptoed off to my own room. Kevin's unique perspectives are often a source of amusement. But that night something else lingered long after the humor. I realized for the first time the very different world Kevin lives in.

He was born 30 years ago, mentally disabled as a result of difficulties during labor. Apart from his size (he's 6-foot-2), there are few ways in which he is an adult. He reasons and communicates with the capabilities of a 7-year-old, and he always will. He will probably always believe that God lives under his bed, that Santa Claus is the one who fills the space under our tree every Christmas and that airplanes stay up in the sky because angels carry them.

I remember wondering if Kevin realizes he is different. Is he ever dissatisfied with his monotonous life? Up before dawn each day, off to work at a workshop for the disabled, home to walk our cocker spaniel, return to eat his favorite macaroni-and-cheese for dinner, and later to bed. The only variation in the entire scheme is laundry, when he hovers excitedly over the washing machine like a mother with her newborn child.

He does not seem dissatisfied. He lopes out to the bus every morning at 7:05, eager for a day of simple work. He wrings his hands excitedly while the water boils on the stove before dinner, and he stays up late twice a week to gather our dirty laundry for his next day's laundry chores.

And Saturdays—oh, the bliss of Saturdays! That's the day my Dad takes Kevin to the airport to have a soft drink, watch the planes land, and speculate on the destination of each passenger inside. "That one's going to Chi-car-go!" Kevin shouts as he claps his hands.

His anticipation is so great he can hardly sleep on Friday nights. And so goes his world of daily rituals and weekend field trips. He doesn't know what it means to be discontent. His life is simple. He will never know the entanglements of wealth of power, and he does not care what brand of clothing he wears or what kind of food he eats. His needs have always been met, and he never worries that one-day they may not be.

His hands are diligent. Kevin is never so happy as when he is working. When he unloads the dishwasher or vacuums the carpet, his heart is completely in it. He does not shrink from a job when it is begun, and he does not leave a job until it is finished. But when his tasks are done, Kevin knows how to relax.

He is not obsessed with his work or the work of others. His heart is pure. He still believes everyone tells the truth, promises must be kept, and when you are wrong, you apologize instead of argue.

Free from pride and unconcerned with appearances, Kevin is not afraid to cry when he is hurt, angry or sorry. He is always transparent, always sincere. And he trusts God. Not confined by intellectual reasoning, when he comes to Christ, he comes as a child. Kevin seems to know God, to really be friends with Him in a way that is difficult for an educated person to grasp. God seems like his closest companion.

In my moments of doubt and frustrations with my Christianity, I envy the security Kevin has in his simple faith. It is then that I am most willing to admit that he has some divine knowledge that rises above my mortal questions. It is then I realize that perhaps he is not the one with the handicap. I am. My obligations, my fear, my pride, my circumstances - they all become disabilities when I do not trust them to God's care.

Who knows if Kevin comprehends things I can never learn? After all, he has spent his whole life in that kind of innocence, praying after dark and soaking up the goodness and love of God. And one day, when the mysteries of heaven are opened, and we are all amazed at how close God really is to our hearts, I'll realize that God heard the simple prayers of a boy who believed that God lived under his bed.

Kevin won't be surprised at all!

—Unknown Author

Are There Dogs In Heaven?

Our 14-year-old dog Abbey died last month. The day after she passed away my 4-year-old daughter Meredith was crying and talking about how much she missed Abbey. She asked if we could write a letter to God so that when Abbey got to heaven, God would recognize her. I told her that I thought that we could, so she dictated these words:

Dear God, Will you please take care of my dog? Abbey died yesterday and is with you in heaven. I miss her very much. I'm happy that you let me have her as my dog even though she got sick. I hope you will play with her. She likes to swim and play with balls.

I am sending a picture of her so when you see her you will know that she is my dog. I really miss her. Love, Meredith

We put the letter in an envelope with a picture of Abbey & Meredith, addressed it to God/Heaven. We put our return address on it.

Meredith pasted several stamps on the front of the envelope because she said it would take lots of stamps to get the letter all the way to heaven. That afternoon she dropped it into the letterbox at the post office. A few **days** later, she asked if God had gotten the letter yet. I told her that I thought He had.

Yesterday, there was a package wrapped in gold paper on our front porch addressed, 'To Meredith' in an unfamiliar hand. Meredith opened it. Inside was a book by Mr. Rogers called *When a Pet Dies.*

Taped to the inside front cover was the letter we had written to God in its opened envelope. On the opposite page was the picture of Abbey and Meredith and this note:

Dear Meredith:

Abbey arrived safely in heaven. Having the picture was a big help and I recognized her right away. Abbey isn't sick anymore. Her spirit is here with me just like it stays in your heart. My mother Mary and your heavenly mother love Abbey and are playing with her right now. Abbey is really smart because he runs to fetch the rubber ball and brings it back to her each time.

Mom cried when Abbey first came to heaven because she knew how sad you were but after she asked me to write back to you and tell you Abbey is safe and happy, she stopped crying. Abbey loved being your dog. Since we don't need our bodies in heaven, I don't have any pockets to keep your picture in so I'm sending it back to you in this little book for you to keep and have something to remember Abbey by.

Thank you for the beautiful letter and thank your mother for helping you write it and sending it to me. What a wonderful mother you have. I picked her especially for you.

I send my blessings every day and remember that I love you very much.

By the way, I'm easy to find. I am wherever there is love

Love,
God

—Unknown Author

Jesus, Help Me to Forgive You

I was the mother of three children and the wife of a wonderful husband. He loved me so much and treated me like a queen everyday. Though I knew I was not that great, Jim would tell me daily that I was the most important person in his life and that he would not hesitate dying for me.

All of my life I prayed for, and dreamed of, marrying a man that I could love and that the fruit of this love and with the help of God, would allow me to bear children and the experience of creating another human being. (In the early summer of 1967, that dream became a reality and Jim and I fell in love and married the following year)

For the next several years our beautiful miracles came along. First to come was my little girl Mary and then Janice only 14 months later and finally John, our bubbling little boy who I knew some day was going to be a famous doctor.

My husband Jim had a great job and we were able to live in a gorgeous home with a little white picket fence circling the one-acre of land. It seemed that all of my dreams had come true within a short time and that God truly answered my prayer.

I could not have been happier, I could never have felt more love than what I now was experiencing and I knew that my life was complete.

All I asked for the remaining years of my life was to be a good wife and a good mother and a teacher of God's infinite love to my children.

The next eight years brought the greatest of joy into my life and I thanked God everyday for the incredible blessings.

One morning, Jim kissed me good by as he left for work and we made arrangements for a date that night. I was to get a baby sitter for 6:00 and Jim would take me out to my favorite restaurant and the dancing to all hours of the night. Jim loved to dance and though I always told him he danced like Jimmy Durante, he knew that he wasn't really a very good dancer. I will say though, -- no one enjoyed dancing more.

I expected my husband home about 5:00 and when the clock hit 6:00 I knew that something was wrong. Jim always called me if he was going to be late.

Finally, at twenty after six, I heard a car pull into the driveway and I ran to the door to greet my husband.

Instead, a police officer came to the door and with tears in his eyes; he told me that a drunk driver had just killed my husband in a car accident.

At that moment, my body drained itself of any life within. I became paralyzed with any emotion and I could not respond nor react to the news with any sense of control as an adult. Finally I was able to call my mother and dad and tell them what had just happened.

It is not necessary to explain what happened next, the funeral, having to tell my children that their daddy was gone and the loneliness that permeated by body every moment I was awake. I knew that I had to do what ever was necessary to give my children the care they needed so desperately, but it was all mechanical and it seemed to drain me of all reality and the real world.

After a few months, the depression over came me and I woke up one morning and walked into the living room and knelt down in front of the picture of Jesus that we always had hanging on the wall above our fireplace.

My exact words to Jesus at that moment was, "I will never forgive You for what You have done to me and my children" You call yourself a God of love. No—You are a God of pain and void of any love. "Because You have power over life and death, You use it at Your will and without consideration of the very lives You created"

Surprisingly, I said these words without tears or any great emotion. My words were deliberate, direct and sincere. God had let me down and I would never be able to forgive what He did to me.

From that moment on, I took the picture of Jesus down from the wall and put it in the basement in a cardboard box.

It's amazing to see that this act of defiance and anger at God seemed to help me cope with my pain and loss and though I thought this bitterness and anger was my lifeline to sanity, it really was my anchor that caused me to cling to despair and emptiness for the next 5 years. Even despite my beautiful children, my life had no meaning.

Though it seemed like a lifetime, five years past by pretty fast and I had finally gained control of my grief and was able to grasp the fullness of life again through the lives of my children and their accomplishments in school and social inner action. I was so proud of them and I knew Jim would have been the proudest father in the world.

As time passed, I knew I would have to talk to God again and try to explain how sorry I was for the words I used about 5 years ago, but I didn't know where to begin.

I decided that church was probably the place to begin because our children were baptized there, made their confirmation, first communion and that is where Jim and I went on occasions when we were very angry at each other. Seemed like healing always found its way at church.

I made arrangements for a sitter so I could attend mass alone and figure out what to say to God and the following weekend I attended mass. I sat in the back pew so I could be unseen, alone and closer to a fast exit should I want to leave in a hurry.

The Gospel reading that weekend was from John 8 1-11 and it told about the woman caught in adultery and how the law of Mosses required the sinner to be stoned to death.

As I heard Jesus say to the woman, "Is there no one to condemn you. Then neither do I. Go and sin no more" my heart burst with regret and remorse for what I had said to Jesus in my grief. At the time I should have called on God for help, was the time I condemned Him for Jim's death and I felt so sorry at that moment.

It wasn't me that needed to forgive Jesus,— it was Jesus from whom I needed forgiveness.

All these years, I had blamed Jesus for the act of a drunk driver. All these years I turned from the only one who could ease my pain. I felt like the woman who had committed adultery and who had just received forgiveness for Jesus—I was undeserving, but the healing was mine just for the taking.

So everyone could hear me, I shouted loud and distinct, "Jesus I forgive you, please forgive me"

My life is now complete again and though I miss my husband more than words could explain, I know that I will be ok. Jesus has forgiven me!

—Unknown Author

Are You Jesus?

A few years ago a group of salesmen went to a regional sales convention in Chicago They had assured their wives that they would be home in plenty of time for Friday night's dinner. In their rush to catch the plane home and with tickets and briefcases, one of these salesmen inadvertently kicked over a table, which held a display of apples.

Apples flew everywhere. Without stopping or looking back, they all managed to reach the plane in time for their nearly missed boarding. ALL BUT ONE! He paused, took a deep breath, got in touch with his feelings and experienced a twinge of compassion for the girl whose apple stand had been over-turned. He told his buddies to go on without him, waved good-bye, told one of them to call his wife when they arrived at their home destination and explain his taking a later flight.

Then he returned to the terminal where the apples were all over the terminal floor. He was glad he did. The 16-year-old girl was totally blind! She was softly crying, tears running down her cheeks in frustration, and at the same time helplessly groping for her spilled produce as the crowd swirled about her, no one stopping and no one to care for her plight. The salesman knelt on the floor with her, gathered up the apples, put them back on the table and helped organize her display.

As he did this, he noticed that many of them had become battered and bruised; these he set aside in another basket. When he had finished, he pulled out his wallet and said to the girl, "Here, please take this $50 for the damage we did. Are you okay?" She nodded through her tears. He continued on with, "I hope we didn't spoil your day too badly."

As the salesman started to walk away, the bewildered blind girl called out to him, "Mister…" He paused and turned to look back into those blind eyes. She continued, "Are you Jesus?"

He stopped in mid-stride. He gently went back and said, "No, I am nothing like Jesus— He is good, kind, caring, loving, and would never have bumped into your display in the first place." The girl gently nodded: "I only asked because I prayed for Jesus to help me gather the apples. He sent you to help me, Thank you for hearing Jesus, Mister."

Then slowly he made his way to catch the later flight with that question burning and bouncing about in his soul: "Are you Jesus?"

Do people mistake you for Jesus? That's our destiny, is it not? To be so much like Jesus that people cannot tell the difference as we live and interact with a world that is blind to His love, life and grace. If we claim to know Him, we should live, walk and act as He would. Knowing Him is more than simply quoting scripture and going to church.

It's actually living the Word as life unfolds day to day. You are the apple of His eye even though you also have been bruised by a fall. He stopped what He was doing and picked up you and me on a hill called Calvary and paid in full for our damaged fruit.

—Unknown Author

Poems that Touch the Heart and Stretch the Imagination

A Star, a Cross, a Reflection of Hope

Out of nowhere it appears like a star in the night, its radiance so bright, a beacon of joy to those who grasp its magnificence of light.

The desire of the mind to see what beholds the truth of creation and the need to understand its purpose.

A vision of a cross, stained with blood, the agony that must be, though no sound can be heard from the beam which holds a promised eternity.

A covenant of faith, creator and the created and then a pause for the mind to absorb the promises foretold.

Can the soul really understand what lies ahead, beyond the darkness and void ahead?

I trust not, for I cannot believe how one would die for the likes of me.

Peace and calm and security now, as the light dims to nothingness and the beam of love illuminates what remains for all to see, a mirror of the heart, a reflection of the soul.

I have seen, I believe!

—Deacon Don Christy

Time Is Endless, God's Priceless Gift

Time is but an accumulation of thoughts and memories in the mind. It spans a lifetime of living, beginning at birth and extends to the moment of conscious realization that immortality is much closer to the future than from the past.

Time also allows us to measure the hopes and dreams of youthful ambitions in an actuality, never fulfilled but still strived for as we grow in wisdom and age. It extends the mind to a personification of God who manifests himself in the subconscious of man so we can acknowledge and prepare for our own pending death.

One's life cycle then is not birth, life, and death as we are led to believe. If this were true, we are to be the most pitied of all creatures. There is a fourth chapter in the book of life that concludes with the resurrection of the body.

The body dies and leaves the home from which it has dwelled, but life itself can never die. Through the soul, which is the essence of all existence, comes the purpose for which we were created.

That purpose is to experience what is yet to come, the unknown, the step in faith that has been revealed to us through the time span of living here on this earth.

What could God's plan be for us if it were not for this reason? What would be the purpose for human existence if not to prepare for the eternal gift of life? Resurrection tells us that. God tells us that!

—Deacon Don Christy

Come, Holy Spirit, Come

Breath of the Holy Spirit, like the wind's quiet whisper.

A reminder of God's presence, silent, without void, and unmistakable.

An awesome experience of magnificent love and never-ending calm.

Brought to the created out of human emotion, never to fail, never to doubt.

A place of conscious effort, understanding what God is about, peace and gentleness, food for the soul.

Grasp its fullness, its meaning, then you have found a heart of love, a spirit of joy.

—Deacon Don Christy

The Weight of Sin

My God, my God, your eyes filled with tears, what have I done through all these years? To hurt you so deeply, to deny your very self, carrying the weight of sin, but never asking for help.

Pain of the cross, unbearable and alone, hanging in shame for sins to atone and for the world to see. A man to die, no need for my sins to hide, for death is final, but life goes on forever.

Suddenly a smile. Tears dried on his face, a peace and calm, pain without a trace. He looks at me through his smile of joy saying, "Do not be ashamed, go on your way and sin no more."

"I have died for you. No greater love could I have shown, it is over now and all in the past, sin in your life has died at last."

"I am God, your Creator, and Jesus is my Son, spirit in splendor and all three as one."

"Asking only for your trust and surrender of love, I seek your goodness and perfection as we join our hearts and become one."

"I in you, and you in me, a bond for all eternity, a life never to cease, for my tears is the love I feel, and my pain is the means to heal, and through that love comes unending peace."

—Deacon Don Christy

God's Presence in A Star

A star racing across the sky, suddenly a shower of light, reflective of God's love and his awesome power and might. A hope comes alive replacing my despair as I see a God who really does care.

His existence is evident; one cannot deny the wonders of creation and his plan for salvation. How can this be? There is no logic in creating a person like me. I was born with sin and continue to fall, and as I reflect on my life, I see no hope at all.

But I gaze again at the star's glitter and light and see the reason for this experience tonight. God is talking to me; he is showing his love through the sky's vastness of space. He reveals a purpose for my life. Feelings of peace and delight now fill my heart as I understand God's reason for my living.

I am to be that shower. I am to be that glitter. I am the hope that streaks across the sky on this night, for God has asked me to tell others about his existence and not waver from the truth and his purpose for life.

I am afraid, Lord, that I will surely fail you, being weak and fragile and sinful in my ways. And yet I hear his voice again, strong and loud and determined as he explains to me, "Fail if you will, Don, but leave that failure up to me. I ask for nothing more or nothing less, just the effort from you to do your best."

And so I attempt to bring God's love to those who do not understand him and who are lost and afraid, knowing that my own failure will be their gain. God told me this; he explained it to me, and we know that God never makes a mistake in his plan for eternity.

I will do my best, Lord!

—Deacon Don Christy

Love Is More than Words

If only words could express feelings about love in a way that others could experience that same feeling, but alas, it cannot be done.

Our love is far greater than words and kind jesters and expressions of gifts and flowers. It is a feeling of total surrender and awe for another person who is able to fulfill the hopes and dreams of our very existence.

It is that moment of joy each time a loved one comes home from work and the peace you feel when you climb into bed together and radiate the warmth through your embrace.

It is the incredible experience of making love and giving of ourselves to each other in wholeness and honest assurance that we are each so unique that no one else can possibly understand.

And finally, it is the realization that God gave us this priceless gift of another because he wanted us to experience heaven here on earth a most beautiful human being created just for me, my soul mate, confidant, and friend. Thank you, Lord.

—Deacon Don Christy

Why, Lord, Were They So Young?

Lord, can you hear us as we cry out Your name? Can You feel our broken hearts exploding with the pain of a tragedy so great that we cannot comprehend our young and innocent whose lives have come to an end?

We stand in disbelief and despair is very real as we try to make sense of this senseless ordeal, a tear from the eye and a heart empty and void. Where were You Lord, as these young ones cried out to You?

They were so young and so full of life; they had so much to offer, and their minds were so bright. They saw the future as a dream to be reached for: a nurse, a doctor, a priest, an author, a pastor, an athlete, all with hopes and all with dreams, those so on fire with life, Your future church, Your creation, the result of Your great might.

Lives destroyed in the blink of an eye, shattered and beaten, shaken and scared, parents who stare into space, looking for their child there.

But they will not see their child will they, Lord? At least for now as they gaze into this space, for You have called them home to be with You, any boy, any girl, any person of any race.

How great your love must be for these whom You called home at such a young age; their life is not over for it has just begun, their time to share with You, to share as one.

Suddenly I hear Your voice as You explain to me the plan You have for all of these destined to live in eternity. Never will I question You again, my Lord; I will never despair, nor will I ever doubt, for my prayers have been answered as I learn what Your plan is all about.

I am Your God, and Jesus is My Son; Spirit in splendor, all three as one. I ask only for Your trust and surrender of your love; I seek your goodness and perfection as we join our hearts. I in you and you in Me, a bond for all eternity, a life never to cease for My own tears are the love I feel and your pain is the means to heal.

It is through this means that comes My unimaginable peace.

—Deacon Don Christy

Why Did God Create Me?

Enough about death! Let us continue our quest for an answer as to why God created you.

Why did God create you? What is your purpose in life? Why is there so much pain in the world? Why? Why? Why?

These are common questions that are asked by everyone at one time or another in their lives. The questions are profound, provocative, and clearly understandable. "I am nothing but a speck of dust in the whole cosmos of creation." "I am insignificant, worthless, unneeded, and unnecessary in the world I live in." "Why me, God?" "Why am I here?"

To begin this search for an answer, we need to understand that we will never truly find the answer. God is a mystery within the very creation of mystery, and as we try to bring him down to our own human understanding of a god, we simply diminish him a little more and create a greater mystery within ourselves.

One thing we can be sure of, God didn't accidentally create us. He didn't make a mistake when he breathed life into our mother's womb, nor did God intend for us to be anything but priceless in his eyes.

How many sleepless nights do we spend thinking about this world and the hundreds upon thousands upon millions of planets there are in the universe and the millions more whose existence we have not even imagined yet? Scientists agree that many of these planets are millions of light-years away from earth, which in itself stretches the imagination beyond our capacity as a human being.

Is there life on other planets, and if there aren't, why would God have such an unimaginable space between each planet and a black hole, which cannot even be defined in terms of distance and vastness of space? What could possibly be the purpose of such vastness just for the earth to exist alone? Is there life on other planets, and if so, did God suffer and die for them as he did for us? Did God go through the same process of crucifixion for others not of this world?

We know that the Immaculate Conception is Mary being born without original sin. Does that mean she didn't need a savior like the rest of us? Would she not be like God incarnate since he is the only one sinless? If she was born without original sin, then how could Mary have had freedom of choice and free will that God promised to every one of his creations? Why, why, why?

Would you be satisfied if I said that God can do whatever he wants, however he wants, and whenever he wants? (I didn't think so.)

Let's try to analyze these wonders in a simple and logical way that only humans can relate to.

> The Most Holy Virgin Mary was, in the first moment of her conception, by a unique gift of grace and privilege of Almighty God, in view of the merits of Jesus Christ, the Redeemer

of mankind, preserved free from all stain of original sin.

—Pope Pius IX

Does it get any clearer than that?

Mary had no need of a Savior. Jesus preserved her from contacting original sin by the saving merits of the cross. God made her a holy vessel to be most fitting for carrying the Holy One someday in her womb. God can save in the future, the present, or the past, and so he is truly Mary's Savior even if he saved her before the rest of us.

The Virgin Mary is not God, but also remember that neither are angels, and yet they are sinless like Adam before he fell from God's graces.

The earth and all that it contains is a mystery that we will not understand until the day we stand face to face with our Creator. In an instant, all will be revealed to us, and we will truly understand God personified. We will no longer have to proclaim "the mystery of faith." The mystery will be ours to grasp and savor as we behold the Son of God in his magnificence.

All of this is fine, you say, but it still doesn't explain why I was created.

That's the easiest question to answer, and so I saved it for last.

You were created because God loves you, and he wants you to love him and worship him. He created you because God only picks the best for his most important jobs, and you were chosen to carry out his work here on earth so that others will come to know him as you now do.

Most importantly, God created you because he wanted you to be part of his life. Are you blessed, or are you blessed? God chose the best!

When you don't know what the Bible says, you don't know what Christ is saying.

Free Choice Free Will

"Faith is not the absence of suffering but is the presence of grace," says President Bush as he addressed the nation.

These are profound words that describe the Christian life today and personify the unconditional love of Christ the Savior.

Can you imagine that God loved us so much that he would not even take away the free choice and free will from the terrorists who flew into the WTC on Tuesday, September 11, 2001?

As a result of this barbaric act, unbelievable suffering and pain was caused for hundreds of thousands of people. In fact, pain and disbelief were felt throughout the whole civilized world and never again would the world be the same.

If it is true that suffering brings grace into the life of a Christian, and I truly believe it does, then it is also true that faith will overcome suffering and replace pain with joy and peace once again.

This is the essence of Christian faith, and each time that suffering comes and goes, it leaves us with a new beginning and a chance to see God's love from a different perspective.

One could relate this "new beginning" to the seasons of the year.

Fall offers a time for reflection and the knowledge of temporary death of nature's creation. Fall is beautiful beyond description as the leaves turn to fire-red and fall gently to the ground in silence.

Winter brings us the yearning of what is to come, and we long for the warmth of summer days ahead.

Spring brings a fragrance and freshness, a new life, and anticipation of beaches and summer vacations to come.

Finally, the arrival of *Summer*, longer days, rest, and gentle breezes, a time to be refreshed while maturing and preparing for the time that it must start all over again.

If we can receive this much joy out of earthly seasonal change, how much more joy will we receive in our new life in Christ at the seasonal change of our soul and the eternal life that waits for all!

I would encourage every person to bring the change of season into the heart of every person God entrusts to you each day!

Imagine the souls that could be saved, the hearts that could be mended, and the suffering we could turn into joy if we would just love a little more, judge a little less, and give more compassion to those who are suffering in this mixed-up world.

His suffering has brought you grace—let this grace bring you new life.

Silence is the vernacular of holiness.

What Is Golden about the Golden Years?

As we enter our final years of life (I am turning seventy in a few months), it is common for us to look back at the years gone by. I think of all the good times in my life and the joys of my existence in a world full of beauty and awesome wonders. I think of my growing-up years with a loving mother and father and their unknown sacrifices to help me acquire success in a difficult world of competition and unprecedented greed.

And then my wife, Donna, enters my life, a woman of grace and beauty—a woman with love bursting at the seams of logic, which says I could never imagine a love so incredible and potent to the senses of manhood. Whether or not I deserve it, God's love brought a woman into my life.

Then came the children, two sons, Scott and Jody, who cannot be described with words sufficient to express my feelings of completeness as a dad.

Through their own love, as they matured and began their quest for the treasures that God had offered to them, they met our daughter-in-laws (daughters we never had), fell in love, and gave us five beautiful grandchildren.

And now as life for my wife and I seems to be winding down and the next generation of the Christy family begins to take shape, I see a purpose for all of the experiences I have had over the years. God was preparing my wife and I for what is guaranteed to come far too fast—leaving this world and entering into the second and most beautiful phase of our created existence, that of eternal life with God.

At the time I am writing this book, and surely before it is published, my ninety-one-year-old mother will have left this earth. Her body is slowly showing signs of shutting down and logically wearing out. Though she is at peace and in no pain as she lives out her final weeks or days or hours, she has expressed her concern to me and asked the question, "Was I good enough to go to heaven?"

I assure everyone she will be in the arms of God soon!

The purpose of this chapter is to reiterate and emphasize why I chose the title of this book to be *Jesus, I Need Your Help!*

Watching my mother lying in her bed day after day, week after week, and month after month, I have come to fully understand the psychological process of dying that an older man or woman is faced with on their own.

No matter how many loved ones are at their side each day, ultimately death is a journey that requires each individual to face alone, head on and with fear of the unknown but anticipation of the joy to come.

Old age can sometimes make us look like a fool, feel like a child, exasperate our sense of the modesty we once cherished.

It can diminish our independence as a viable, productive creature.

My mother described old age while living in a nursing home as the following:

- Old age stole my dignity, my independence, and my self-worth.

- My hands are no longer soft. (They used to be soft and smooth.)

- My eyes now have trouble seeing all of the beauty I once enjoyed so much.

- My legs no longer carry me from place to place, and though I thank God for a wheelchair, I no longer see purpose of moving about.

- My ears no longer hear the voices of my loved ones, and I am not good at reading lips.

- The visits from those who continue to love me in my old age are precious, but my will to talk amid my fragile and tired state will not allow me.

- I know I cannot continue to exist without food, but my mind won't allow me to eat enough to sustain life.

- Sometimes I get a burst of energy that lasts only a few minutes, and then I say to myself, "What is the use?" and I lie back to sleep again.

- The baths I receive are forced and cold, and I have given up the fight to resist.

- No longer knowing my financial condition, I hope for the best but fear the little money I had is now gone for my own medical care. (Why do I need money any longer I ask myself?)

- Though I see my loved ones often, I still feel lonely and of no value, and I fear they don't understand.

- I miss being hugged by my husband, Bud.

- He died and left me alone after fifty-two years of married life. (I would give up a million years of living just to have him hold me again for only a minute.) Oh God, I miss him!

- I pray that my children do not think of me as crabby or senile or unappreciative of all they do for me. I am just so weak that I can't make myself respond to their loving ways.

- Inside this old body still lies a pretty girl, as I once was and hope to be again.

- Take me home, Lord, when you will, and please return the patience I have lost as I wait for you.

- I am not afraid. I am at peace. I am *ready*!

Jesus, I Need Your Help!

My mother died peacefully only four weeks after this book was completed and is now with our Lord in paradise.

Conclusion

It is time to end this book and allow the reader to contemplate the words of the Holy Spirit: "It is not your words that you speak, but it is that of the Holy Spirit speaking within you."

If you have read this book in its entirety and have been inspired by any of its contents, then you must know that it was not my words that inspired you. It was not my ideas that caused that hint of emotion deep within your soul, nor was is that small twinge of fear that caused you to rethink your spirituality and your relationship with God.

On the contrary, it was the voice of the Holy Spirit whispering gentle thoughts of agape and asking you again to stop seeking him so vigorously. He has already found you!

God bless you for taking the time to hear God's message of love and his instruction on how to live a fulfilling and peaceful life that is free of financial problems filled with peace in the heart and rest for the soul.

It is the knowledge of what is to come that gives us the absence of fear for the future.

May our Lord bless you and keep you. May his light shine on you and be gracious to you and may Almighty God bless you in the name of the Father and of the Son and of the Holy Spirit, amen.

About the Author

The author of this book, appropriately titled, *Jesus, I Need Your Help* is Deacon Don Christy. He was ordained into Holy Orders of the Catholic Church twenty years ago, and as you will discover through his writings, Deacon Don offers new ideas about life as a Christian and explains  why it is okay to struggle and even doubt your faith.

Deacon Don, along with his wife, Donna, are the parents of two sons, Scott and Jody, two daughter-in-laws, Jennifer and Kim, and five grandchildren, Mike, Nicole, Rebecca, Nate, and MacKenzie.

Because of Deacon Don's extensive experience, he is a sought-after motivational speaker and has given numerous keynote addresses to organizations such as St. Vincent de Paul Society, Health and Human Services, Women's Christian organizations, and hundreds of seminars and workshops on Christian financial budgeting and spiritual counseling.

Deacon Don is the founder of Alpha Omega Residential Rehabilitation Facility, a home for released inmates suffering addiction problems, and serves as a chaplain at the local correctional facility.

His wife, Donna, assists him in Project Rachael, counseling for the post-abortion sufferers, and offers spiritual counseling for troubled marriages.

Because of Deacon's personal experience of a life-changing and miraculous event in Medjugorje, Yugoslavia, your heart will be touched, your faith will be strengthened, and your understanding of the humanism of Christ and his Mother Mary will take on a new perspective.

His writings come from deep within the heart, his insight and honesty allows for a down to earth solution for spiritual problems and, as a Christian and ordained deacon, he shows a deep and genuine love and reverence for his vocation in the Catholic Church.

And your life will change forever.